Built to Last?

REFLECTIONS ON BRITISH HOUSING POLICY

SECOND EDITION

EDITED BY JOHN GOODWIN & CAROL GRANT

First published in 1992 by ROOF magazine, Shelter, 88 Old Street, London EC1V 9HU

Reprinted 1994, 1996. Second edition 1997

British Library Cataloguing in Publication (CIP) Data
A CIP catalogue record for this book is available from the British Library

ISBN 1-870767-58-6

Printed by Russell Press, Radford Mill, Norton Street, Nottingham NG7 3HU

Cover design by Saul Chester
Cover photographs by Saul Chester and Jon Walter

Design by Michaela Chandler of Posters Unlimited

Acknowledgements

This second edition of *Built to Last* could not have been produced without the time, energy and enthusiasm of its many contributors, listed overleaf. Special thanks are due to Carol Grant, who edited the first edition and wrote the Foreword to this edition, and to Peter Malpass, who had the original idea for the book – and who has contributed four chapters to this edition. Peter Williams also gave much advice on the original format and style of the book, as well as contributing a new concluding chapter.

Thanks are also due to the members of ROOF's editorial board for their advice and support, and to the ROOF staff who helped with the production and marketing of the book: Julian Blake, Julian Birch, Tim Dwelly, Nicole Charlett, David Dropkin and John Whitmore. Indexing was by David Morgan.

John Goodwin – September 1997

Contributors

Ron Bailey is the parliamentary officer for Friends of the Earth and for the Association for the Conservation of Energy

Julian Blake is the editor of ROOF magazine

Martin Boddy is the director of the Centre for Urban Studies at the School for Policy Studies, University of Bristol

David Clapham is the director of the Centre for Housing Management and Development at the University of Wales, Cardiff

Seán Damer is a sociologist and writer from Glasgow

John English is a lecturer in social policy at the Department of Applied Social Studies, University of Paisley

Janet Ford is the director of the Centre for Housing Policy at the University of York

Ray Forrest is professor of urban studies at the School for Policy Studies, University of Bristol

John Goodwin is the deputy editor of ROOF magazine

Carol Grant is the director of communications at the Local Government Association

Sara Hill is a research associate at the Public Health Research and Resource Centre, University of Salford

Peter Kemp is the director of the ESRC Centre for Housing Research and Urban Studies at the University of Glasgow

Stuart Lowe is a lecturer in social policy at the University of York

Peter Malpass is professor of housing policy at the University of the West of England in Bristol

Robin Means is reader in social gerontology at the School for Policy Studies, University of Bristol

Alan Murie is the director of the Centre for Urban and Regional Studies, University of Birmingham

Martin Pawley is an architectural writer and critic

Janet Richards is the manager of the Chartered Institute of Housing's Good Practice Unit

Susan Smith is a professor of geography at the University of Edinburgh

Paul Spicker is a senior lecturer in social policy at the University of Dundee

Mark Stephens is a lecturer at the Centre for Housing Research and Urban Studies at the University of Glasgow

Jerry White is the local government ombudsman for central and south-west England

Peter Williams is the deputy director general of the Council of Mortgage Lenders.

Contents

Foreword

Carol Grant

Most of the articles in this book were originally commissioned for ROOF's 'Second Take' series, which began nearly ten years ago. As the authors were writing, the 1988 Housing Act brought major shifts in housing policy. Councils were being replaced by housing associations as the main providers of new social housing. The private rented sector was deregulated. Home ownership continued to grow, and the housing market boomed.

There have been many changes since then, and since the collection of articles first appeared as *Built to Last* in 1992. A new government has inherited a complex housing legacy. Councils remain the biggest source of new lettings, housing poorer people in a stock with a huge backlog of repairs. Housing associations, now 'registered social landlords', have become complex financial institutions. The house price bubble burst, and 'negative equity' entered the language of housing. The homelessness legislation, so fundamental to the rights of homeless people, has been repealed.

ROOF is an editorially independent magazine published by Shelter. Through the magazine, its sister supplement ROOF *Briefing*, regular debates and books, its strength has been to put housing policy into a social, political and economic context, to challenge existing orthodoxies and to develop new ideas. It has been *the* journal of record in housing in the last decade.

The shelves are stacked with weighty books on housing history. The Second Take series, although written mostly by housing academics, was designed to offer something different – readable pieces of social history that had relevance to today's housing practitioners, students and general readers. Since the pieces were originally collected into *Built to*

Last, the book has been through two reprints and has sold thousands of copies.

This edition has been significantly expanded, with many of the original pieces updated, and new chapters added on housing tenure, home ownership, and the recent developments in housing associations' and building societies' structure and finance.

I was delighted to edit the first volume, and to have been part of the team that developed this new edition. Thanks are due to my colleagues on the editorial board, for providing the ideas and creativity that make ROOF such a refreshing read. Thanks are also due to the ROOF staff, and John Goodwin in particular, for undertaking the hard work of commissioning and editing the new material. And I am grateful to all those who bought the first edition and proved that there is demand for such an important book.

ROOF's role in publishing this book is to educate, to entertain and to stimulate those interested in housing to think about how their current views and practices have been shaped by the experience of earlier generations. To develop and implement housing policies that work, and that meet the diverse range of modern housing needs, we have to build on a firm foundation of knowledge. Only then will Britain have a housing policy that is Built to Last.■

Carol Grant is the director of communications at the Local Government Association and is a former editor of ROOF

Homes and castles

Stuart Lowe

Was it historically inevitable that Britain would become a nation of home-owners?

By the end of the 1980s, a long process of tenure change finally came to its conclusion. Britain became firmly established among a club of nations dominated by home ownership. One hundred years of transition saw a huge demographic shift. At the end of the 19th century, over 90 per cent of the population lived in privately rented homes. Yet few other countries in Europe experienced such a marked change. So why did Britain diverge from the mainstream of Europe in its housing tenure and become a nation of home owners, while countries such as Germany and France retained larger rental markets?

The main explanation focuses on events before, during and after the trauma of the first world war, and the way working-class housing was developed early in the 20th century. In Britain, private renting gave way to a public rental system run almost exclusively by municipal authorities – with a rigid demarcation developing between the two forms of renting. This split is an important part of the reason behind the growth and eventual dominance of owner-occupation. In France, Germany, Austria, the Netherlands and Scandinavia, rented housing did not segment in this way, and home ownership is just one part of a truly mixed housing market.

There was, in my view, no inevitability to this divergence. Political processes and strategies made a huge difference, despite being often short-term and pedantic responses to problems of the time. To understand this, it is helpful to balance the detailed administration of

Built to Last?

Long view: Why did home ownership become the dominant form of housing tenure in Britain? Elsewhere in Europe a much higher proportion of homes is privately rented – in Britain private landlords were squeezed between private housing and owner-occupation

Nick Dawe

policy against the background socio-economic 'wash'. Think, if you like, of a water-colourist painting detail onto already coloured paper.

For the first stage of the tenure picture, we need to sketch in some details about the events that overtook private landlords in Britain during the latter part of the 19th century. Then, they were increasingly subject to financial pressures from local taxation and new standards of building control administered by public health officials. The humble local by-law was of particular significance because, from 1858, local authorities were able to control speculative builders by insisting on certain minimum standards (for example, window sizes, air spaces in roofs and, externally, road widths). These by-laws helped to control the spread of back-to-back dwellings, and further legislation in the mid-1870s enabled authorities to compel developers to deposit plans for inspection and amendment, and allow site inspection.

Compared to their European counterparts, private landlords in

Britain were at this point relatively powerless politically. Most were small-scale owners of a few properties which they held as investments. Small property owners were represented neither by the emerging Labour movement, the Conservative party (with its essentially rural-elite character) or the Liberals, whose basic instinct was to tax land ownership. In the gathering recognition of the need for state subsidies, at least to solve short-term problems, private landlords were ill-equipped to play a part in shaping events. They were not a popular class and wielded little influence in the power plays of domestic politics around the first world war.

So one of the central reasons for the decision to mass-build council housing was that private landlords did not have a social or political base from which to argue their case, particularly over the provision of subsidy. It was already clear – well before the first world war made it inevitable – that the provision of working-class rental housing would require funding from the state. Walter Long, the Conservative local government spokesman, was considering a number of ways of subsidising the programme before the war.[1] A Royal Commission on 'The housing of the working classes' had laid a foundation for this extraordinary conclusion as early as the mid-1880s. It was equally apparent before the war that the scale of provision of housing by subsidised finance was going to be very considerable, even if, as was thought at the time, it was a temporary measure. A figure of 120,000 new houses was being discussed before 1914.

Clearly it was unlikely that private landlords would be the prime recipients of the large subsidy implied by these plans. They were a politically weak and fragmented class whose market position had been undermined by the changing economic conditions of the late 19th century.

North of the border, the situation was even worse. As Seán Damer shows in Chapter five, Scottish landlords were reviled. In England, the position was less controversial. One of the reasons for this was that tenancies in England, unlike Scotland, were based on a simple weekly let, which allowed flexibility (but also poor security of tenure). Powers of summary eviction were rarely used – even in cases of late payment of rent – because it took a minimum of 28 days to secure an eviction, with a consequent loss of rent. However, English landlords did

3

little to endear themselves either to the government or to the population at large during the war.

There are three possible explanations for central government's choice of local authorities to lead the crash housebuilding programme. First, the trusts and model dwelling companies had to be excluded from the strategy because they were not easily plannable. Despite their achievement in building some 50,000 dwellings up to 1914, they were heavily concentrated in the London area and could hardly be responsible for a national programme of building. By contrast, although on a smaller scale, many municipal authorities in the north as well as in London had experimented with building rental housing – often to a high standard.

Second, as already explained, private landlords' profitability was hit by public health legislation and the implementation of local by-laws. So there was a certain irony in the choice of local authorities to spearhead the building programme – they were more used to policing the building of new homes and, as a result, there were 'housing officers' in every area of the country. In order to overcome their reticence, a very generous subsidy was offered in the famous Addison Act of 1919.

Third, a rather more 'broad-brush' part of the canvas is the question of the class character of English society. Private landlords were a *petit bourgeois* class and were politically weak. But the working-class movement developing at the end of the 19th century was finally becoming stronger; its identity essentially reformist in outlook and parliamentary in tactics.

The British working class was the first such class in world history. It had suffered a series of defeats at various times, struggled heroically, but ended the century exhausted and bowed. Unlike many of their European counterparts, the British Labour party was established with the single intent of representing trade unions in parliament. The state was regarded to all intents and purposes as class neutral, both nationally and locally. This was a quite different response compared to, say, the German unions, who regarded the state with suspicion. The British 'parliamentary road to socialism' tended to exclude alternatives such as housing co-ops or directly provided trade union-sponsored housing, which were common on the continent.

The importance of housing in the politics of the time can be seen in the experiments with social housing provision made in cities such as Liverpool and Sheffield, where the Labour party made very early gains and was a significant political force well before it succeeded on the national stage with the formation of the 1924 government. In Sheffield, for example, a design competition led to one of the earliest garden suburbs being built by a municipal authority (the Flowers Estate at Tinsley, so called because all the streets were named after flowers) with cottage-style architecture rather than the more familiar terraces. The relationship between central and local government was important to the long-term establishment of council housing as the alternative to private landlordism – for example, state subsidies were not mandatory and it required local impetus to take them up.

So it came to be that the British rental sectors divided into two quite distinct forms, public and private. On the one hand, the private landlords were not able to be subsidised. On the other hand, council housing provided an entirely viable and manageable alternative form of provision. The commitment to council housing and, crucially, the lack of any real alternative is deeply embedded in this early history. Elsewhere in Europe – in Paris, Berlin, Vienna, Budapest, Stockholm – a much more plural system of housing the working classes emerged at this time. It often incorporated private landlords as well as other agencies; trade unions, co-ops, housing associations, employers, local councils, the national state itself.

This period, particularly the 1920s, is central to the *divergence* that took place in European housing. Britain went down its unique municipal route, with almost nothing else of significance happening until housing associations flourished following the 1974 Housing Act. Unsubsidised private landlordism was unable to compete, except perhaps for a short time in the mid-1930s on the back of the speculative building boom.

From an early stage in Britain, the new public rented housing and the private rented sector were rigidly demarcated by financial arrangements, management systems, access criteria and degree of public accountability. Elsewhere there was a much more mixed system. In some cases, notably in Germany, Austria and later Sweden, this mixing was the basis of a more 'harmonised' rental market in which the public and private divide was much less rigid and the rental sectors operated in competition with each other. This is what Jim Kemeny calls a 'unitary' rental market.[2] The two housing tenures retained their identities, but competed with each other – keeping rents controlled at affordable levels by demand and with the public sector often setting local market prices. These countries retained viable rental sectors which were part of a more diverse housing market in which home ownership did not become dominant by default.

Of major significance in Britain was the subsidy system. Not only were private landlords excluded from subsidy, but the nature of the subsidy offered to local authorities – based on 'historic cost' calculations – caused the breach between the sectors gradually to widen. Once again we are back to administrative detail which can have a profound influence on outcomes. Local authorities were offered a 'bricks and mortar' subsidy – so much per dwelling built, paid annually into the authority's housing revenue account (following the 1930 Housing Act) over 20, 30, 40 years or even longer. In essence, each dwelling built attracted a revenue stream of subsidy payments and rental income. It was a system devised by central government to entice the authorities to build and allow them to keep rents below market levels – referred to in legislation as 'reasonable' rents. This system competed directly with the unsubsidised private sector from the very beginning. The 1919 Addison Act resulted in the construction of over 170,000 council houses, the so-called 'homes fit for heroes' (although very few soldiers could afford to live in them). It also became *increasingly* competitive, because as the costs of building and loans were paid off, so local authorities owned debt-free housing stock. This implied that rents would *decrease* over time, taking into account management and maintenance costs.

So one of the unintended consequences of the early decision to boost council housing was the creation of a maturing stock of low-rent dwellings. Without subsidy, the private sector could not compete, because higher rents were needed to raise a return on investment sufficient to attract capital into the sector. This process – which Kemeny calls the 'maturation' of council housing – drove a wedge between the private and public rented sectors. This was lethal to the prospects of private landlords and made it difficult to see how the sectors could at some future stage become more closely connected as they were in some other European nations.

By the time council housing reached its peak in the early 1970s – when nearly one third of households were council tenants – the maturation of the stock was so significant that some kind of policy response was inevitable. But the problem was that the private rented sector had shrunk to a fraction of its previous size. Expensive high-rise council flats built in these latter stages of the council house era were supported by the older, low-debt stock through a cross subsidy. Even so, it might have been feasible to enable the public sector to influence and shape the private rental market.

Instead, the competitive advantage enjoyed by the public sector was destroyed by a succession of governments from the mid-1970s on. The strategy was simple. Rents were to rise in line with the residual private market according to orthodox 'capital value' accountancy, sales of council houses were to strip out whole sections of the public rental stock and historic cost subsidies were terminated (by the 1980 Housing Act). And so home ownership came to have a monopoly in housing provision as both rented sectors diminished. State managed vandalism on this scale is probably only surpassed in modern times by the rapid privatisation of large sections of state housing in the countries of the former USSR and its East and Central European satellites.

Virtually every comparative housing book written in the last five years refers to the recent growth of home ownership in Europe and argues that it is the consequence of a convergence of ideas drawn in essence from Thatcherism and US-style real estate market theory. However, there is little evidence to support such an explanation. As we have seen, in many European countries the rental tenures are at the heart of these housing systems. The public and private sectors work in partnership and are often not particularly distinguishable from each other. Home ownership works alongside the rental tenures and it seems likely that any growth in owner-occupation arises not from an aggressive political agenda, or some kind of osmosis from Britain, but is simply a readjustment in the relationship between the tenures in mature, multi-tenure housing systems. Reading back on the histories of Germany, France, the Netherlands, Austria and the Scandinavian nations suggests that rental tenures are solidly placed at the core of their housing markets, are not in decline and have not been sacrificed on the altar of home ownership.

In Britain, families are locked into a rigidly demarcated and highly unbalanced market in which certain kinds of choices have been systematically removed. We are owners (or mortgagors) or tenants in a residual public rental sector and there is very little crossover between the two systems, although recent research has shown very considerable mobility *within* the main housing tenures.[3] This pattern of rapid mobility inside sectors and a relative lack of mobility between them is symptomatic of a highly dysfunctional British housing system.

The historic advantage of low debt in the older council housing stock could have been turned to a social purpose – the creation of more plural and truly competitive, cross-sector housing.

But the chance for Britain to turn in the direction of some of our European neighbours has now been lost – probably for ever. The consequence of course is that home ownership has come surging through and, in the absence of any competition, now enjoys an unstoppable monopoly position. The rest, as they say, is history. ■

Notes

1. J Morton, 'The 1890 Act and its aftermath – the era of the model dwellings', in S Lowe and D Hughes (eds), *A new century of social housing*, Leicester University Press, 1991

2. J Kemeny, *Housing and social theory*, Routledge, 1992

3. R Burrows, *Contemporary patterns of residential mobility in relation to social housing in England*, Centre for Housing Policy, research report, 1997

Stuart Lowe is a lecturer in social policy at the University of York

chapter 2

Business out of charity

Jerry White

Were the early charitable housing trusts a philanthropic response to housing need, or a hard-headed use of capital to quell working class unrest?

Housing associations have their origins in the 1840s, that troubled decade of famine in Ireland and 'the hungry forties' in the rest of Britain. This was the era of revolutions across Europe and Chartism and riot at home – with hastily armed volunteers patrolling the Bank of England to protect it from popular pillage.

The appearance of the housing association movement at that turbulent time was no accident. The beginnings of housing associations are deeply rooted in class relations and in the nature and function of the British state. The shadows cast by those origins remain plainly visible today (see Chapters 16 and 20 for their more recent history).

The middle-class public of the 1840s was bombarded as never before by information, both reportage and statistics, on working-class living conditions. Public health reports, newspaper 'special correspondents' and novelists all provided detailed and sometimes lurid exposure of Liverpool cellars, stilt dwellings in Bermondsey's Jacob's Island, dung heaps as high as houses in Bethnal Green, Glasgow 'wynds' and courts so narrow you could touch the high buildings on both sides by stretching out your arms. Drainage, water supply and sanitary dwellings became the urgent concern of middle-class reformers and the new local government structures organised around public health.

Pity for the poor undoubtedly spurred on rich men and women to do something to remedy the conditions they read about. The first housing association is said to have been the Metropolitan Association for Improving the Dwellings of the Industrious Classes, formed in 1841, but not building actively until a few years later. The busiest of the first associations, the Society for Improving the Conditions of the Labouring Classes, was part-founded by the Earl of Shaftesbury, an evangelical christian and tireless social reformer. Prince Albert, not the last royal with an interest in housing reform, became its president, and its first tenement dwellings were built in Gray's Inn Road, London, for 50 households, 30 of them single people. One of the society's first ventures, in nearby Bloomsbury, still stands as a monument to the humanitarian ideals of the very first housing associations.

The 1860s saw the flowering of the housing association movement with City alderman (later Sir) Sydney Waterlow's dwellings in Finsbury, followed by his formation of the Improved Industrial Dwellings Company; and by the donation by the American merchant George Peabody of £150,000 (rising to £500,000) to the poor of London in 1862.

Peabody's gift – which was to be a thorn in the side of the capitalists who saw housing associations as a business – was the single greatest act of charity of his day. The Peabody and Waterlow tenement block dwellings were to help change the face of London's old City suburbs of Finsbury, Shoreditch, Bethnal Green, Southwark, Holborn and Westminster over the next 40 years.

In the face of such munificence it might seem carping to remember that humanitarianism does not exclude self-interest. It is clear that, from the very earliest days, bourgeois philanthropy expressed through the housing association movement was rarely disinterested. Housing associations were seen to benefit the middle classes too – not, of course, by providing cheap dwellings for them, but in the social benefits which improvement in working-class living conditions brought.

Housing reform was seen as a cure for crime in areas like Spitalfields, where churchgoers needed police protection from bag-snatchers and 'hooligans'. It was a cure for pauperism through drink and other causes, and for infectious diseases like cholera and smallpox which would not recognise the boundaries between poor and prosperous neighbourhoods. And it helped quell political unrest. 'Ay,

Joseph Rowntree Foundation

Domestic bliss: parlour house in New Earswick, Joseph Rowntree's model village in York

truly,' Shaftesbury enthused after a meeting to publicise the work of his Society in 1848, 'this is the way to stifle Chartism'. This explicit political purpose was no doubt prominent in the minds of philanthropic employers who devised model villages for their workers, like Salt, Cadbury, Rowntree, Akroyd and others in the 1850s and 1860s.

Capitalist speculation in working class housing had, of course, a long history but also, by the 1840s, a bad reputation. Landlords were exposed as house-screwers, house-jobbers, rackrenters and slumlords in the 1840s, as they were to be again by the Royal Commission on the Housing of the Working Classes in 1885. But from the earliest days, some housing associations were consciously seeking to make capital investment in working-class housing respectable. This aspect of the movement has often been called semi-philanthropic and the name is well-chosen. There undoubtedly was a charitable element in choosing this way to invest money rather than, say, railways, imperial ventures, or slum property. But the investment opportunities offered by the associations were not insignificant. The Metropolitan Association of 1841 was set up on these 'strict business principles' to yield five per cent per annum on capital invested – not a bad return in those less usurious times. And in the years to follow, a good number of associations took this road – explicitly capitalist, but with charitable hedgerows.

Waterlow's company in the 1860s eventually raised £500,000 capital, after considerable mistrust from investors who did not believe a charitable enterprise could be made to pay. It was followed by the Artisans' Labourers' and General Dwellings Company, formed in 1867 and specialising in cottage estates. But the main era of the semi-philanthropic housing associations was the 1880s, with a rediscovery of the housing problem and renewed fears of political unrest, especially in London. The East End Dwellings Company, the Four Per Cent Industrial Dwellings Company, and the Guinness Trust were the biggest semi-philanthropic associations to emerge in that decade.

The 1880s also revealed the tensions within the movement between the charitable organisations, represented pre-eminently by Peabody, and those on the capitalist road. Arguments arose particularly over the state-inspired disposal of slum clearance sites in central London. The semi-philanthropists claimed that Peabody, without investors' interests to safeguard, could afford to outbid other companies for the best sites. It could afford to build to higher standards, attracting those tenants – policemen, clerks, railwaymen – best able to pay. This was one reason why investors were hard to come by and why the greatest problem of the semi-philanthropic associations was shortage of capital. In the final outcome, private investment was inadequate to solve the working-class housing problem, even with the state playing the role of enabler.

Until 1919, the British state consciously stood back from the working-class housing problem. A post-war period of considerable unrest provoked a definitive interventionist response which was to characterise housing policy until 1980. But the role of the state before the first world war had stopped well short of public housing provision. Although the Housing of the Working Classes Act 1890 had allowed for rate-borne building by local authorities, only a few took the opportunity. Prior to that, councils were generally stopped from building for rent. When they cleared slums they had to dispose of the assembled sites to a developer who would build working-class housing on them. The role of developer in this context was adopted by the housing associations – both capitalist and charitable wings.

The key piece of legislation which enabled housing associations to play this role was the 1875 Artisans' and Labourers' Dwellings Improvement Act – known as the Cross Act after the reforming Tory home secretary who introduced it. This gave urban councils the power to clear 'unhealthy areas' by buying the houses compulsorily, evicting the tenants, demolishing the buildings and clearing the site. But when the site was empty the local authority could not build dwellings – although it could lay out sewers and streets for those who would. The site then had to be sold on to the association, which undertook to build dwellings for the same number of people (but not the same people) who had been evicted in the first place.

In this way, housing associations were made the executors of state policy. In inner London, they built nearly 10,000 flats on Cross Act slum clearance sites, virtually all between 1878 and 1890. Between 1840 and 1905, associations built 40,000 dwellings in Greater London – this can be compared with the combined efforts of all London local authorities before 1914, who built just 13,000 homes.

Until 1919, then, housing associations were in the front line of state-inspired housing provision and were widely seen as the major providers outside private speculative development. But the inadequacy of this provision was starkly apparent – fewer than 1,000 dwellings a year in Greater London, for instance. And it was inadequate in one other respect too. For it became increasingly apparent that, despite early intentions, it was not 'the poor' who were benefiting from housing associations at all.

Providing improved housing was an explicit form of social imperialism for the early housing association reformers. Octavia Hill probably represented most consciously their reforming zeal. For her the urban working class was to be colonised in the same way as Aborigines or Zulus in a different context. 'Truly a wild, lawless, desolate little kingdom to come to rule over', she wrote of an early experiment in buying a slum court in west London and improving the houses. 'On what principles was I to rule these people?' the 'Queen of Marylebone' asked herself. 'Firstly, to demand a strict fulfilment of their duties to me – one of the chief of which would be the punctual payment of rent; and secondly, to endeavour to be so unfailingly just and patient that they should learn to trust the rule that was over them.'

Built to Last?

Hill's system of intrepid visiting by lady rent collectors, with the bailiffs as their stormtroopers, was applied not only in her own schemes but by other associations also. In the 1880s, Miss Cons kept the tenants of Surrey Buildings in check 'with that peculiar mixture of sympathy and authority which characterises the modern class of governing women'.

But this sort of controlling influence, exhausting no doubt for all involved, could not be sustained for long. More and more housing associations took the easy way out. Instead of reforming difficult tenants, especially those too difficult to pay their rent, they would get rid of them. Beatrice Webb, a rent collector on the Hill system for a time in Wapping, put it succinctly in her diary entry for 4 June 1885: 'Working hard. Buildings unsatisfactory. Caretaker hopelessly inadequate. Tenants, rough lot – the Aborigines of the east end. Pressure to exclude these and take in only the respectable – follow Peabody's example. Interview with the superintendent of Peabody's. "We had a rough lot to begin with, had to weed them of the old inhabitants – now only take in men with regular employment."'

Thus the poorest were excluded from the shelter envisaged in Peabody's gift to 'the poor'. Housing associations relying on making a dividend for their investors had even more reason to follow suit. When the Four Per Cent Industrial Dwellings Company developed a Spitalfields site in 1886-87, letting most of the new flats to Jewish immigrants, they turned the class make-up of the area on its head. The old slum houses had as tenants street sellers, rag and bone dealers, labourers, dockers – 70 per cent unskilled labour. The new flats were occupied by tailors, cigarette makers, cabinet makers, even a few policemen – 70 per cent skilled.

Housing associations, then, had borne the main burden of building improved housing for working people – although not the poorest – before the first world war. But they were to lay dormant during the war years while central government for the first time became active in building homes for munitions workers in Woolwich, Dumfriesshire and Cumberland.

After 1919, it was local authorities, not housing associations, who were entrusted with the task of building a mass programme of 'homes fit for heroes'.

In the inter-war years, housing associations made little contribution, at least in terms of the numbers of new dwellings built, to the housing drives of successive governments of every political complexion. The Victorian philanthropic and semi-philanthropic trusts mainly retrenched into managing their pre-1914 stock rather than building anew. Some trusts ceased to expand when the men and women who had inspired them retired or died. But a small number, based more on the Peabody philanthropic endowment model rather than those relying on shareholders' capital, continued as developers. Even so, the big four trusts (Peabody, Sutton, Guinness, and Samuel Lewis) completed between them just 8,324 new dwellings in Greater London from 1900 to 1939. Yet from 1919 to 1939, in the same area, local authorities built over 153,000 dwellings, and the private sector put up 619,000 – most of them suburban semis. In this context, the housing association contribution was marginal at best.

Yet the big trusts don't tell the whole story of the housing association movement in these fallow years. Out-gunned as they were by mass local authority provision, small 'public utility societies' flourished, especially in inner London. By 1934 there were 14 of these societies in the capital, calling themselves variously 'housing associations', 'housing societies', 'improvement societies' or similar.

The best known was the St Pancras House Improvement Society Ltd, active in Somers Town and run by the redoubtable Irene Barclay. It was the first association to register as a non-profit-making limited company under the 1893-4 Industrial and Provident Societies Acts. The Society raised subscriptions through the personal influence of its members, like Father Basil Jellicoe, a local high churchman. Subscribers could also take a share of stock paying a 2.5 to 3 per cent dividend (about the same return as offered by government bonds at the time).

The society and its imitators were able to develop a more sensitive and personal touch than the local council in buying and clearing slum property and rehousing virtually all the original tenants in new flats. The public utility societies may have perpetuated the class dichotomy of the Victorian trusts – the well-heeled and well-connected providing improved dwellings for the poor. But, at a time when the poor were blamed less for their poverty, they were more tolerant of misbehaviour or rent arrears than in Octavia Hill's golden days.

So, despite the penetration of local authorities into the working-class housing market during the 1920s and 1930s, housing associations held onto their old niche and developed a new one. The big trusts confined themselves to management rather than development, but they were joined by a flourishing community of smaller local societies, buying up old houses in streets their members knew thoroughly, and replacing them with well-designed modern accommodation for the people displaced. They, rather than their Victorian forebears, were to be the shape of things to come – at least until the era of mergers and takeovers half a century or so later. ■

Jerry White is local government ombudsman for central and south-west England

Victorian values

Paul Spicker

A century ago, Charles Booth undertook the first major social survey of London. His work made a clear link between housing conditions and poverty

It is over a hundred years since the first volume appeared of Charles Booth's *Life and labour of the people in London*. It was the beginning of a series of 17 volumes, finally completed in 1903. The study began with a close examination of poverty in London. It developed into detailed examinations of every type of occupation, religious influence and municipal effort.

This was probably the first major social survey of the way that people lived, undertaken with a daunting comprehensiveness. Although Booth presented his work as a kind of census, it was much more. It used a range of methods to bring the study to life.

He described his work as a sort of 'photography' – a striking metaphor for 1889. The observations are at times stark, sentimental, provocative, and moralistic – Booth was very much a man of his time. The work had a major impact, for it provided the basis of the arguments for the introduction of old age pensions, and directly influenced the subsequent analysis of poverty.

Booth began by obtaining reports from school board visitors about the condition of poor families. Initially, he and his investigators avoided going into the houses themselves, considering it to be an 'unwarrantable impertinence' to 'meddle' with people's lives but, as the survey progressed, he wrote: 'We gained confidence, and made it a rule to see each street ourselves at the time we received the visitors' account of it.' The picture that eventually emerged was a thorough analysis of London, street by street, with an assessment of the poverty and social class of the inhabitants.

The types of housing were graded mainly according to the degree of poverty of the people who lived in them, rather than the quality of the housing itself. The areas were graded by colour, so that their distribution could be plotted on a map. The worst areas were coloured black on the maps. They were overcrowded and insanitary. 'In little rooms no more than eight feet square, would be found living father, mother and several children... Not a room would be free from vermin, and in many life at night was unbearable... Most of the doors stood open at night as well as all day, and the passage and the stairs gave shelter to many who were altogether homeless.' The notes on households in black streets were given in the greatest detail. One example, somewhat abridged, will have to suffice:

'The story of the first floor in this house is one of the utmost horror. A man whose name I will not even pretend to give, by trade a sweep, having three grown-up sons, lived with and abused a woman to her death. She was an orphan brought up in an industrial school and had lived with him at least 11 years, having one child by him. She was good to the other children, as well as to her own child, and kind to the man. Wife and mother in every sense, except legally. But he so knocked her about that she was never free from bruises... The man had regular pay – 25s a week – and would spend nearly all in drink. He would swear at her, and kicks and blows would follow... She was got into a refuge, but he coaxed her back with fair words, with what results?... A few weeks later the poor woman lay on her bed unconscious, with blackened eye and face all bruised. She was dying... There was no prosecution, the neighbours shielded the man, and he too is now dead.'

The next class of houses were dark blue with black lines; the houses bore 'the look of great poverty'. For example:

'No. 7 Rydal Street: upper. Three rooms, four persons. Man, wife and two children. Labourer (nominal). A family of professional beggars. Always moving to escape rent. Lazy and filthy.'

Or: 'No. 6 Cleveland Terraces. Four rooms, seven persons. Man, wife and five children. Was in gasworks. Met with an accident and now cannot work. Clean respectable people. Great poverty.'

Museum of London

Dark blue houses had a poor environment, with large houses often subdivided into many smaller units. Of one street, Booth commented: 'The people who dwell here look as poverty-stricken as the houses.' People such as the residents of 'No.1 Latin Place South. Cottage. Rooms two, Persons eight. Man, wife and six young children. Gardener, out of work. Wife lately confined. Semi-starvation. Is helped by charity.'

Or: 'No. 2 Latin Place South. Cottage. Rooms two, Persons five. Man, wife and three young children. Paralysed. Wife does mangling. Dreadful poverty.'

The better grades of property where poor people lived were light blue, purple and pink. A light blue street could still be judged 'rough and untidy', the houses 'ill cared for and shabby', like: 'No. 4 Little Merton Street. Two rooms, four people. Man, wife and two daughters. Cab-washer. A drunkard. Beats his wife and was in prison for it. Wife out late. Daughter wild.'

Purple streets contained a mixture of poverty and adequate housing. 'No. 38 Gordon Road. Six rooms, two persons. Old man and wife. Tailor, but crippled and paralysed. The wife was a school mistress.

Are fairly well to do. Take a lodger sometimes.

Pink streets were adequate, but they were not without their problems. Many old people, and families where there was unemployment, disability or widows, still appeared as poor:

'No. 43 Martin Street. Three rooms, four persons. Man, wife and two children. Blind. Has pension. Wife washes but is getting too old for it. Just manage. Poor.

'No. 23 Chesterfield Street is occupied in two rooms by a seaman and sailmaker, with wife and three children. He works at his trade half the year, and goes to sea the other half. Is sometimes badly off. Two of the children go to school, and the other is partially paralysed.'

The conclusions from the study were clear. Poverty was much more prevalent than it had been believed to be – nearly a third of the population of London was poor – and, although Booth was ready to blame many poor people for their own poverty, there was also much poverty that arose without fault.

For Booth, housing conditions and poverty were closely linked. He defined poverty as a condition in which people had resources which were barely sufficient 'for a decent independent life'. Housing conditions were the clearest indication of people's material resources, because it showed what they were able to afford. Labourers, whose income seemed to be sufficient to have adequate housing, for example, lived in worse conditions than might be expected because their incomes were not secure, and they could not afford a more expensive commitment. Booth put a great deal of emphasis on the importance of overcrowding as an indicator of poverty. As the research went on, he began to dismiss other evidence that people were poor if they were not overcrowded, although major problems were evident in the early part of the survey through the incidence of sickness, disability and old age.

The maps revealed a distinct pattern of poverty in particular areas. It was clear to Booth that poor people lived not just in bad housing conditions but in poor areas. He refers, for example, to one area as 'a district where poverty is almost solid'. Some part of this was attributable to the social reputation of the area: 'A row of houses falls into bad repute, due merely to a few undesirable tenants who, if they are not ejected, render the neighbourhood too hot for anyone with a taste for decency.'

The judgement suggests that the tenants were 'bringing down' the area. But Booth did not, despite the received opinion of his time, and his own substantial prejudices, blame bad areas exclusively on the habits of the poor. Rather, he saw it as a combination of factors. One explanation which he favoured for the concentration of poverty was simple: people with adequate incomes were able to move out and improve their circumstances, poor people were not. But there are many other comments contained in *Life and labour*, particularly in the later volumes, about different influences on the spatial pattern of particular areas. For example, he notes at one point the effect of the layout and design of estates: 'In Battersea, poverty is caught and held in successive railway loops south of the Battersea Park Road... This is one of the best object-lessons in "poverty-traps" in London.'

It would be going too far to suggest that Booth had a clearly worked out model of the city, or of the processes through which such problems emerged. Booth's skill was as an observer; he recorded what he saw, believing that 'the facts' would speak for themselves. The importance of his study was that it revealed so much about the conditions people lived in.

The comprehensive approach of the survey meant that there was a great deal within it about the specific problems of housing, though this was not the central focus. Booth's work was unusual, for example, in trying to make an adequate assessment of the circumstances of single homeless people. He began with a study of common lodging houses – hostels as we would now call them – though he argued that homelessness in such cases was an issue of lifestyle: 'From the luxury of the west end residential club to the "fourpenny doss" of Bangor Street or Short's Gardens is but a matter of degree.'

In Booth's day, there were over 30,000 people in this type of accommodation in central London; although there was a wide range of incomes, it disproportionately housed the poorest. Homeless people tended to move between lodging houses and sleeping rough. Unable to take a complete census, he took two samples from night shelters, including details of their age, employment, marital status and ethnic origin. Booth put special emphasis on a count taken after a long frost, when few people would be sleeping rough, but he was dissatisfied with the quality of the information, and he regretted that he could not supply more.

Built to Last?

The main area in which the survey directly considers housing is in a discussion of blocks of flats, which were graded in relation to light, air and sanitation. Of one building, a four storey block graded 'very bad', there is the following comment: 'Everything is filthy, and the stench very bad. A few more steps lead to a dark passage with two-roomed or four one-roomed tenements. The floors above are similar. A notice outside tells passers that there are 'rooms to let, painted and papered, and in good repair' and that 'none but quiet respectable people need apply'.

Much of the material on blocks of flats was contributed by Octavia Hill, who wrote a section about their 'influence on character'. Hill tended to dismiss the importance of facilities and sanitation in favour of improving people's characters. To some extent, this runs counter to the survey's strong emphasis on poor physical conditions. However, her criticisms of flats as an environment for families were picked up by Booth in the final volume, and many of the reservations about this form of living still ring true.

When, at the end of the survey, Booth reviewed his material, he felt able to make some more general statements about bad housing. He described 12 classes of bad housing: Old housing in bad condition; new housing that was badly built; property neglected by the owners; property abused by the current occupiers; housing with insufficient space; housing on damp or rubbish-filled ground; 'houses occupied by families of a class for which they are not designed and are not suited'; insanitary houses; badly arranged blocks; badly managed blocks; housing with excessive rents; and crowded homes.

Booth showed that he was aware, in a way that later commentators were not, that bad housing was not a simple issue. It was, rather, a combination of condition, design, management, social factors, and the use of the property. His analysis might have provided the basis for a reconsideration of housing policy for poor people. Sadly, unlike the material on poverty, it was to have virtually no discernible influence at all. Much of the current debate on poor council estates is going over the same ground – to the point where Booth's analysis seems relatively sophisticated.

It is difficult to say whether there is much to learn now from Booth's work. No-one would want to take on what he said uncritically, and many of the important points he made have been made again since. However, there are a number of valuable insights. Some are historical. Booth's survey reminds us of the vices of an unregulated private market – why public housing was necessary, and why private renting started to die off.

There are object lessons in the experience of life without an adequate system of social security benefits or health services. The study shows, too, that the link between poverty and poor areas is long-standing, and that it applied in a very different housing market from that which we have now. Local authorities have been blamed for creating 'ghettos'. But the ghettos existed long before the local authorities started to build.

There are, besides, a number of observations in the study about poverty which seem, in retrospect, well-founded. First, poverty, for many people, is all-embracing. Problems of one type are strongly associated with problems of other types. Second, although poverty tends to be concentrated in poor areas, it is not confined to them. It is found in many places. Third, poor areas develop for a variety of reasons, including the pattern of industry, the type of housing, the reputation of an area, and the power of the residents to choose.

The power of the study stems not from its judgements or arguments, but the weight of material it accumulated. The evidence in Booth's study reinforces, and in many ways anticipates, an understanding of poverty which has taken a century to develop. ∎

Paul Spicker is a senior lecturer in social policy at the University of Dundee

chapter 4

A woman of her time

David Clapham

The work of 19th century housing reformer Octavia Hill has
attracted praise and condemnation in almost equal measure

Although Octavia Hill was not the originator of housing
management, she brought it to the forefront of debate on social
reform. Her recognition of the importance of the need for trained
housing workers laid the groundwork for the creation of the housing
management profession.

As an activity, housing management existed long before Hill
started her housing work in Paradise Place, Marylebone, in 1865.
However, it was carried out mainly by professionals such as house
agents, auctioneers and surveyors, who all vied for pre-eminence. For
many, housing management was simply another source of income to
supplement their main activity.

Hill has continued to enjoy substantial prominence since her death
(the headquarters of the Chartered Institute of Housing in Coventry, for
instance, is called Octavia House). But she is a controversial figure who
has, in recent years, attracted both unstinting praise and aggressive
condemnation from writers who have considered the relevance of her
work to current problems. Hill was very much a woman of her time,
and to advocate the use of her methods today is to misunderstand the
context within which her work took place. The social context of
housing work today is very different from the one she faced.

In the early 19th century, the pressures of industrial
development, rapid population growth and the consequent poor living
conditions in cities enlivened charitable enterprise. State involvement
in social affairs was almost non-existent, in accordance with the

Octavia Hill: social reformer, philanthropist and early housing manager. 'There are two main principles to be observed in any plan for raising the poorest class in England,' she wrote in 1869. 'One is that personal influence must be brought strongly to bear on the individuals. The other is that the rich must abstain from any form of alms giving.'

Ruskin Gallery

prevailing liberal attitude of *laissez-faire*. Philanthropy was also encouraged by a rise in evangelical christianity which combined a strong emphasis on personal sacrifice and good works with an obsession with individual depravity. It also established a belief in the family as the paramount social institution and a desire to bring christianity into the home. Thomas Chalmers, an influential Scottish religious reformer of the time, argued that the aim was to restore the social values of the countryside to large urban communities by giving the poor the kind of neighbourly supervision and assistance that would develop in them qualities of self-reliance and independence.

Thus, most parishes had their sewing classes and mothers' meetings, as well as 'visiting societies' to reach the homes of the poor. The focus on the family and the home meant that women were thought to be particularly well-suited to charitable service. 'From their domestic citadel, they [women] made ever wider forays into society as the front-line defenders of family life.'[1]

State involvement in welfare in the mid-19th century was largely through relief provided under the 1834 Poor Law Amendment Act, and, in the case of the 'able-bodied' poor and their families, it meant the workhouse. As this was meant to be a last resort, conditions were spartan enough to deter all but the destitute. The poor were generally categorised into the 'deserving' and the 'undeserving'. Charitable effort was concentrated on the 'deserving', those who conformed to the moral values of the day and were prepared to exercise 'self-help' to deal with their problems, whilst the 'undeserving' were consigned to the care of the poor law. Philanthropists set out to avoid, at all costs, pauperising the poor – creating a dependence on handouts. 'Indiscriminate' relief was frowned upon and the emphasis was on visiting the poor in their own homes to spread christian values through individual contact and to provide practical help and advice on running the home and habits of cleanliness. 'In Britain they [philanthropists] sought to reform the family through a moral and physical cleaning of the nation's homes'.[2]

Octavia Hill was born in Wisbech in 1838. Her father, James Hill, was a merchant who was associated with many radical liberal causes of the time and endorsed the co-operative ideas of Robert Owen. Her mother, Caroline Hill, was the daughter of Dr Southwood Smith, a leading sanitary reformer, and contributed some radical writings on education. From an early age, Octavia was surrounded by talk of social reform and had contact with many of the leading social reformers.

When Octavia was in her early teens, her father suffered a breakdown in health brought on by the collapse of his business. Caroline Hill and her family were left with no income and with business debts to repay. Caroline took Octavia and some of her sisters to London where they were forced to earn their living. Unlike most Victorian philanthropists, Octavia was dogged by personal financial insecurity until the later stages of her life. In London, Octavia worked as the supervisor of a toy-making workroom for poor children and experienced at first hand their atrocious living conditions. It was also during this period in London that her religious convictions grew. She was much influenced by the teaching of F D Maurice who, like many other reformers of the time, placed emphasis on helping the poor through personal contact and decried any form of indiscriminate charity, which he claimed would breed dependency.

Built to Last?

These ideas were accepted by Octavia Hill and rigidly adhered to in all her subsequent work. She wrote in 1869: 'There are two main principles to be observed in any plan for raising the poorest class in England. One is that personal influence must be brought strongly to bear on the individuals. The other is that the rich must abstain from any form of alms giving.'[3]

Octavia's ideas then were not original, but reflected contemporary thinking about social reform. Her disquiet at the habits of the poor, gained from her experiences with the children in her workroom and their families, was matched by a disapproval of the behaviour of many landlords. She criticised them for not keeping their properties in good repair, for permitting overcrowding through sub-letting and for allowing arrears of rent to accrue. She longed to show that if a landlord's duties were carried out in a businesslike way, it would be possible to provide reasonable conditions and yet still make a reasonable return on investment. Housing reform could thus be achieved without charity or public subsidy from the tax- or rate-payer.

At the same time she saw management of houses as a means of making personal contact with the poor to 'urge them to rouse themselves from the lethargy and indolent habits into which they have fallen'.[4]

Hill got the chance to implement her ideas when a friend, John Ruskin, was persuaded to buy some properties in Marylebone and install her as manager. The properties (and most of her subsequent ones) were in a very poor state of repair when she took them over. Sanitary facilities were inadequate and often dilapidated. Windows were broken and covered with rags and paper. Rooms were overcrowded, sometimes damp and had plaster falling from the walls and fire-grates collapsing into the room. Overcrowding was rife and large arrears of rent were common. The tenants were the poorest who could afford their own room – Hill never attempted to house the very poorest. When rooms became vacant they were improved, and tenants who showed signs of responding well to her requirements were offered them.

Other improvements were carried out only when tenants were deemed to deserve them and they could be paid for out of a surplus from rents. Overcrowded families were encouraged to take on extra rooms when they became available, and sub-letting was forbidden. Eviction was threatened if arrears of rent were incurred, or if tenants did not otherwise meet Hill's standards. Tenants of low moral standards – the 'undeserving' poor – were summarily evicted, and she records one case where a man was threatened with eviction if he did not send his children to school.

The key to Octavia Hill's 'system' was the personal relationship between landlord and tenant. She tried to re-create in urban areas the traditional paternalism of the country landowner. Her visits to collect rent were seen as opportunities to develop personal respect and friendship, to offer support and advice, and occasionally offer material help where this would not pauperise the recipient. She employed some of the older girls to scrub the stairs in order to give them experience of work and to foster a sense of pride in the property. She also employed some of her male tenants to carry out repairs to the property, holding back jobs to help tide them over periods of unemployment.

Hill adopted many contemporary philanthropic activities. She tried to find some communal space in her blocks which could be used for sewing classes, mothers' meetings and other charitable work. She tried to provide areas for children to play (under the watchful eye of a supervisor to organise their games) and to provide some greenery to brighten up her tenants' lives.

Hill was successful in improving the conditions of the properties in her care whilst making a five per cent return for the owner. She also claimed to have helped many of her tenants 'improve' themselves, although it would be interesting to know what her tenants felt about her efforts. As news of her work spread, she was offered more properties by contemporary bodies such as the Ecclesiastical Commissioners. She recruited volunteers to manage the properties for her and trained them in book-keeping, sanitary science and landlord and tenant law as well as in the practical skills of dealing with tenants. They were also required to be familiar with the activities of other agencies working for the poor.

Hill was adamant that the key to her work was a set of principles, not a detailed system. Therefore, she operated in a very decentralised way, with her workers being given their own properties to manage and the flexibility to meet the principles in their own ways.

Built to Last?

The principles which underpinned Octavia Hill's management method also determined her increasingly sought-after views on contemporary issues. She was influential in the drafting of the 1875 Artisans' and Labourers' Dwellings Improvement Act (the Cross Act) which gave local authorities the powers to purchase and demolish 'unhealthy' areas of unfit housing. She also gave evidence to the Royal Commission on the Housing of the Working Classes in 1884.

Hill's views on housing reform were built on her principle that the management of houses should go hand in hand with social work with the tenants. 'You cannot deal with the people and their homes separately...the people's homes are bad, partly because their habits and lives are what they are. Transplant them tomorrow to a healthy and commodious home and they would pollute and destroy them.'

For this reason she was highly critical of the activities of many of the model dwelling companies (the other major form of philanthropic housing activity) for not placing enough emphasis on personal contact with tenants. Also, she criticised their pre-occupation with the building of new blocks of flats with good sanitary facilities, quite rightly arguing that this form of provision was out of the reach of the poorest and worst-housed families. Therefore, she was in favour of the improvement of existing properties to minimal standards in order that a poorer class of tenant could be helped. She also criticised the model dwelling companies for the building of large blocks of flats, which she considered detrimental to family life, rather than cottages.

Hill reserved most criticism for the idea that councils should build and manage housing. Like most contemporary philanthropists, she had a profound distrust of the state. She felt that public subsidy for housing was indiscriminate, and would pauperise the poor. She also disliked the idea of tenants being able to vote for their landlord through local elections – an arrangement which she held was open to abuse.

Towards the end of the 19th century, Octavia Hill began to look increasingly out of step with the times. Her dislike of state involvement placed her in a policy backwater as the state moved inexorably deeper into housing issues. Also, the social and economic conditions of the time meant that she felt herself unable to guarantee a return of five per cent to owners of property, and so her approach began to seem less viable. Octavia Hill was undoubtedly a woman of strong personal qualities which qualify her to stand alongside the other great women philanthropists of the age. Her work was not confined to housing; her love of the countryside led her to become one of the founder members of the National Trust.

Her passion for social reform also led her to take an active and leading role in the Charity Organisation Society which, through its personal visiting of the poor, was the forerunner of modern social work practice. This work led to her being appointed to the Royal Commission on the Poor Law which sat between 1905 and 1909.

It is difficult to assess Hill's contribution to housing. She offered little new thinking on social reform as she was heavily influenced by the contemporary ideas of others, but her original contribution was to link concern for reforming the poor with the management of housing. Her ideas on housing policy were sought-after and respected, but were increasingly ignored. It is interesting to speculate, however, whether subsidies for housebuilding, often discussed in the early years of the 20th century, might have been introduced before 1919 had Octavia Hill supported rather than vehemently opposed them.

Through her practical work she was able to improve the housing conditions of a significant number of people, although it is impossible to estimate how many, because with her devolved system of responsibility she was unable to work out the number of properties managed under her method. Whatever the number, however, it was clearly very small in relation to the total number of households. Her influence on model dwelling companies and on private landlords and managing agents was minimal. Her prominence was out of all proportion to the size of the practical contribution she made.

Octavia Hill's management method has exerted a continuing, if limited, influence over housing management practice. With the growth of council housing after the first world war, the management task was usually split between a number of existing local authority departments and was seen as an administrative activity rather than as a means of reforming the poor. Hill's ideas were kept alive by the Society of Women Housing Estate Managers (later to merge with the Institute of Housing) formed by her supporters and with a membership largely confined to the voluntary sector. Some local authorities adopted the Octavia Hill system and appointed women 'visitors', but they were in a small minority. However, although the ideas were not widely implemented by local authorities, they survived and resurfaced at times of concern about housing management. For example, the Central Housing Advisory Committee, in its investigation of housing management in 1935, received evidence from Octavia Hill's supporters, and gave guarded support for their work.

Four factors have led to a renewed interest in Octavia Hill's ideas in recent years: the predominant concern with the management of existing stock rather than with development issues; the increasing concentration of poor people in the public rented sector; the emergence of hard-to-let estates; and the acceptance in some political quarters of the need for a return to Victorian values.

Advocates of Octavia Hill's approach, such as Anne Power, claim that the basic problems facing housing management today are 'strikingly similar in many ways to those of the late 19th century'.[5]

However, even strong advocates express reservations about Hill's firm christian beliefs and her authoritarianism based on a particular set of moral values. Octavia Hill was adamant that what were worth following were the basic principles which her management system was designed to achieve, rather than the system itself, which she recognised would have to be flexible to meet changing circumstances. Undaunted, some present-day advocates promote her management method, but reject the principles underlying it.

Others reject both Octavia Hill's principles and her method, and blame her influence for most of the perceived problems of housing management. For example, Paul Spicker blames her for the continuing over-use of eviction as a management tool; the over-emphasis on cleanliness; and for widespread grading of poor tenants into deserving and undeserving. He argues that Hill's moralistic and authoritarian approach is inconsistent with, and undermines, current ideas of basic rights to welfare, which he argues underpin the modern welfare state.[6]

Advocates and opponents make the mistake of over-emphasising Octavia Hill's personal contribution. She evidently had remarkable personal qualities. But her work was based on social principles which were widely held at the time. Support for, or criticism of, Octavia Hill's approach tends to imply comment on Victorian society itself or to be based on the misguided belief that her management method, and the principles on which it is based, can be uprooted from their context and transported forward to a completely different set of political, social, economic and institutional circumstances.

The true value of a study of Octavia Hill's principles and methods is not in their current applicability but in the questions raised about housing management which are relevant to the current situation.

For example, the close association in her work between social work and housing management raises questions about the current role of the latter, with the concentration of disadvantaged people in the public rented sector and the government's commitment to community care. Should housing management adopt a more welfare-orientated role than at present, or at least improve its links with social work?

Hill's authoritarianism and her intention to use housing management to control and change the behaviour of tenants leads to interesting questions about the role of housing management today with a trend towards a much stricter enforcement of tenancy conditions, and the involvement of housing managers in crime reduction initiatives. Finally, Octavia Hill sometimes employed her own tenants to carry out work on her properties in order to help them over difficult times. In the current context, this raises interesting questions about the integration of housing and economic development.

These are important questions which a study of Octavia Hill's work raises, but each generation of housing managers has to find its own answers in ever-changing circumstances. ■

Notes

1. F Prochaska, *The voluntary impulse – philanthropy in modern Britain*, Faber and Faber, 1988
2. Ibid
3. G Darley, *Octavia Hill – a life*, Constable, 1990
4. O Hill, *Homes of the London poor*, Macmillan, 1875
5. A Power, *Property before people – the management of twentieth-century council housing*, Allen and Unwin, 1987
6. P Spicker, 'Legacy of Octavia Hill', *Housing* magazine, June 1985

David Clapham is director of the Centre for Housing Management and Development at the University of Wales, Cardiff

chapter 5

Striking out on Red Clyde

Seán Damer

Glasgow's celebrated rent strike gave rise to 70 years of rent control – and demonstrated the power of working class communities in Scotland to defeat unpopular measures

Popular culture in Scotland has long reflected a hatred of landlords and their agents (known as 'factors'). In 1784, Robert Burns wrote in the *Twa Dugs*:

'I've noticed, on our Laird's *court-day*,
An' mony a time my heart's been wae,
Poor *tenant-bodies*, scant o' cash,
Hoe they maun thole a *factor's* snash*:
He'll stamp an' threaten, curse an' swear.
He'll apprehend them, *poind*** their gear,
While thy maun stand, wi aspect humble
An' hear it a', and fear an' tremble!'
(* :*abuse*)
(** :*seize*)

Such popular feeling towards property owners and their factors in the city of Glasgow stemmed from the fact that a substantial proportion of the city's population historically came from the Highlands of Scotland. They were dispossessed people, victims of the ruthless land clearances. They had every reason to bring bitter feelings towards landlords with them, and these are expressed in many songs and poems, and in the oral culture of the Gaels.

Similarly, an even larger section of Glasgow's population came from Ireland, penniless victims of the 1840s famine and the later land wars. The Irish too were bitter against the landlords who had thrown them off the land, and again this was expressed in song. Such a population, grossly overcrowded in Glasgow's slum tenements, was a very volatile one.

The property owners of Glasgow and their factors were organised in powerful cartels which dominated the private rented market, the biggest housing sector in Glasgow until the second world war. In the decades before the first world war, they were utterly ruthless. The Scottish legal system was on their side, and armed them with a galaxy of legislation which they did not hesitate to use – warrant sales, arrestment of wages, evictions.

Factors also issued a 'line' or reference to their tenants, and this was a powerful weapon for controlling tenants who complained about the disrepair of their houses, or who objected to exorbitant rents. Lack of a line meant that no factor in the city would grant a tenancy in a decent tenement house, and so the unfortunate tenant would be driven to seek accommodation in a slum.

It was the factors who bore the brunt of popular discontent about this system as they were the people who dealt with the public on a day-to-day basis. The antipathy felt towards them by working-class people can be gauged from the stories in the annual Christmas pantomimes in Glasgow at the turn of the century. In every single one, the factor, 'Mr Money Bags', is a figure of derision.

In the first couple of decades of this century, the records of the sheriff courts show a staggering annual list of applications for warrants for 'ejectment' – eviction, arrestment of wages, poinding and warrant-sales. 'Poinding' (pronounced 'pinding') meant seizing and selling the goods of a debtor. The 'law of urban hypothec' in Scotland said that a tenant's 'furniture, furnishing, and tools are liable to sequestration by a landlord immediately after they enter on possession of a house as security for rent not then accrued, due, or payable'. Failure to pay the rent, or failure to pay the full term of the rent in advance, gave the landlord or his factor the right to act. And they did.

The tenants of Glasgow fought back in every way they could, and rent and housing issues dominated Clydeside working-class politics from the start of this century. Local tenants had the legal right

Glasgow rent strike

Glasgow People's Palace

Battle ground: In the first two decades of this century, Glasgow saw a series of battles between landlords and tenants over rents and evictions. Matters came to a head in the Glasgow rent strike of 1915, which started when landlords used the scarcity of accommodation to increase rents

to lodge an objection against a warrant or eviction, and this they did in their thousands, actively encouraged by John Wheatley, Mary Barbour and Andrew MacBride of the Independent Labour Party-inspired Scottish Labour housing association.

Women would pack the stair when a sheriff-officer came to carry out an eviction and make it impossible for him to move. Sheriff-officers were often pelted with rubbish, or thrown into the midden, the communal refuse heap in the backcourt of the tenements. Similarly, if the sheriff-officers came to execute a warrant sale, to forcibly sell the tenant's goods in order to pay arrears of rent, locals would pack the sale, buy their neighbour's things for a pittance, and drive off dealers and outsiders with threats of violence.

In the case of evictions, and particularly during the protracted rent strike in Clydebank during the 1920s, neighbours would put the evicted person's furniture back into the house and re-occupy it. The ultimate weapon tenants had against grasping factors was to do a 'moonie', a moonlight flit, and this was a common occurrence.

Matters came to a head in the celebrated Glasgow rent strike of 1915. With thousands of men away at the front, the city was flooded with munitions workers from elsewhere in Britain. The factors took the opportunity of this monopoly on scarce accommodation to raise rents. There was immediate uproar.

The Glasgow Labour Housing Association called an immediate rent strike, and soon whole streets in the city were displaying placards in their windows: 'Rent Strikes Against Increases: We Are Not Removing.' The housing association, in conjunction with local women, organised street committees to ensure that the strike was solid, and to resist any attempts at eviction for non-payment of the increased rent. The housewives were equipped with handbells to ring should a sheriff-officer be seen, and would physically pack the stair to prevent the eviction being carried out.

But the factors' greed was such that they took some rent-striking Govan shipyard workers to the sheriff court to get their wages arrested to pay off the arrears of rent. This was a move of monumental stupidity. The women of Govan went down to the yards and brought the men out. The word went round like wildfire. Thousands of demonstrators converged on the sheriff court. A delegation of workers told the sheriff-officer that if he convicted the rent strikers, there would be a general strike on the Clyde the next day. Faced with such a possibility in Britain's main munitions-producing area in the middle of a war which was not going well, the government caved in.

A Rent Restriction Act was rushed through parliament which froze rents at the pre-war level. This was a major victory for the working-class movement. In spite of numerous efforts on the part of property owners to remove it, the principle of rent restrictions was firmly established, and was to remain in force for the next half century. It was the beginning of the end of the arbitrary power of factors and property owners in Glasgow.

These issues were a part of everyday experience in Glasgow until the second world war; they fuelled the Red Clyde movement and informed all aspects of local working-class culture. They were also a central part of the experience of local women, for it was they who had to manage the household budget, deal in the affairs of the stair and street, resist eviction, threaten dealers at warrant sales, and cope with the factor's snash. It would be hard to underestimate the depth of feeling on Clydeside on these issues.

And yet, in 1990, Strathclyde regional council did just that. Marx once said that history repeats itself, the first time as tragedy, the second time as farce. What went on in 1990 with the poll tax verges on the farcical.

When the poll tax was introduced, the Labour party went along with it, even to the extent of drawing up the legal machinery for putting the detested poinding and warrant sales into operation. This resulted in massive popular disgust.

By July 1990, a third of Glasgow's population had refused to pay the poll tax – well over 200,000 people. In March, Strathclyde regional council issued 145,000 summary warrants in the city. The local anti-poll tax campaign was exceptionally well-organised, and distributed information sheets telling tenants their rights and providing hot-line telephone numbers. They drew on the lessons of Glasgow's history, saying that the letters sheriff-officers sent out informing tenants of an impending warrant sale were terrorising them into paying the poll tax.

In various 'at risk' neighbourhoods, there were mobile patrols with mobile phones ready to organise should a sheriff-officer be spotted on his way to carry out a warrant sale. Modern technology replaced the handbells used by the women of Glasgow in 1915 for exactly the same purpose. In a manner strikingly reminiscent of the 1915 rent strike, ordinary Glaswegians learnt that the only way to resist the poll tax was to organise themselves in their neighbourhoods, keep in touch with other areas and be on the alert.

As the millennium approaches, with New Labour now in power with a handsome majority, and as there will now be a Scottish parliament, these kinds of lessons might appear redundant. This is doubtful. As local councils have been both starved of cash and hamstrung by regulations over nearly two decades of Tory government, so the key issue in council housing is now repairs. And nowhere is this more true than in Scotland's older council housing schemes. The problems of these schemes appear intractable with many having upwards of 70 per cent of tenants on housing benefit. Two solutions are currently being aired. The first is the formation of housing companies and the second is the formation of housing associations. Quite apart from the important issue of who controls these housing companies, it is highly unlikely that private finance is going to be interested in older, more rundown schemes like Glasgow's four peripheral estates, or Dumbarton's Bonhill.

And, while housing associations are much-vaunted in Scotland, they actually constitute only four per cent of national housing stock, and carry proportionately very high staff costs. In this respect, they are a privileged sector of the housing market, not a prototypical solution. Further, Scottish council housing tenants are well-informed and well-organised. Some Clydeside tenants associations are already organised against housing companies despite what either the Chartered Institute of Housing or the Labour government recommend. It is hard to resist the conclusion that the lessons of 1915 are still relevant north of the border, and might well have to be applied in the not-too-distant future. ■

Seán Damer is a sociologist and writer from Glasgow

chapter 6

Our mutual friends

Martin Boddy

How, and why, did building societies grow from humble 18th century self-help organisations into major providers of housing loans by the time of the second world war?

The building society movement is thought to have been born in 1775, with the founding of a small society at the Golden Cross Inn, Birmingham. Others soon followed in the Midlands and the North. The very first building societies were mutual, self-help organisations established to meet the housing needs of better-off working-class migrants to the rapidly expanding industrial towns. The Longridge building society, set up near Preston in 1793, listed among its members weavers, yeomen, stonemasons, a carpenter and a cotton spinner.

Legal recognition of building societies as corporate bodies, distinct from banks or companies, came with the 1836 Building Societies Act. It was the 1874 Building Societies Act, however, following an 1872 Royal Commission, which provided what was to be a remarkably durable framework for societies' later expansion.

In the early days, a small group of members would meet regularly, at first usually in an inn. As regular investment or 'subscriptions' built up, they allocated to each member in turn the value of a standard 'share' in the society. This was typically £150, around the sum required to buy a house. Practices varied. Some of the early societies, rather than paying out funds as a lump sum, in effect acted as developer. They would themselves acquire land and organise the building of houses, which were then allocated to members – hence 'building societies'.

The order in which members received their 'share' or house

might be decided by drawing lots. In other cases, members bid for shares, paying a premium – a form of interest – on top of the nominal value, which served to swell the society's funds. Members who received their share or house first obviously continued paying in on a regular basis. Subscriptions continued until all members had received a lump sum share or a house. The society then terminated.

These early 'terminating societies' soon started accepting money from investors to speed up the rate at which funds available to members accumulated. Loans were repaid, with interest, out of members' subscriptions. It was from this that the modern 'permanent' building society, with separate investing and borrowing members, rapidly evolved.

Investors could deposit and withdraw funds. Borrowing members were granted loans, repayable with interest over a set number of years. And, since societies no longer had to terminate once all founder members had received their share of the accumulated funds, the way was also open for the longer-term expansion of individual permanent societies. First recorded in 1845, permanent societies rapidly expanded in number and grew in size, soon outstripping the original 'terminators', which died off early this century.

Many present-day societies can in fact be traced back to the earliest permanent societies. It was the development of permanent societies that really marked the origins of the modern building society movement. As an 1872 Royal Commission put it, the growth of the permanent societies 'altogether changed the character and altered the sphere of the building society movement'.

There were three important changes. First, societies rapidly took on the modern character of financial institutions, albeit specialised on the lending side in the housing sector. In fact, to the Royal Commission, they appeared little different in some respects from banks. They appeared to be 'mainly agencies for the investment of capital, rather than for enabling the industrious to provide dwellings for themselves'.

Second, the term 'building society' was already largely an historical curiosity. In the words of the commissioners, then, as now: 'Building societies do not build, they simply make advances on

Halifax plc

Extra help: a hometown branch of the Halifax, later Britain's biggest building society, in the 1920s

building. They are in fact investment associations, mainly confining themselves to real property.' A significant part of their lending was to individuals buying houses for owner-occupation. Loans to developers and landlords building or buying houses to rent out were also common, and continued into the early 1930s. Lending to landowners, housebuilders and even, early on, industrialists, was not uncommon.

Third, the management and boards of directors of these rapidly expanding and complex institutions was soon professionalised, and taken over by the educated *bourgeoisie*, shaking loose the societies' working-class roots.

In the late Victorian period, societies increasingly turned their backs on the demon drink. Some met in the more sober atmosphere of temperance halls and non-conformist school rooms. Others, such as the Halifax, started early on to acquire office premises from which to operate, and the local aristocracy and worthies filled the boardroom. Liberal and non-conformist connections grew. The modern *Building Societies Gazette* received start-up funds from the non-conformist journal *Christian World*.

Much discussion in the Royal Commission report focused on the issue of whether societies should enjoy some form of legal status as corporate bodies, distinct from banks or limited liability companies. Was there any justification for maintaining such differences, or could they simply register as a bank or company under the relevant Act?

It was a debate reminiscent in many ways of discussion around the 1986 Building Societies Act. This allowed societies to convert to public limited companies (of which much more in chapter 22). The 1874 Act came out in favour of separate legal status. It made a distinction between the 'mutual' nature of the societies based on 'membership' and the profit-orientated character of banks and companies owned collectively by their shareholders.

It was a dubious distinction, even at the time. Mass membership permanent societies bore little relationship to the cosy, self-help image of the early organisations. But separate corporate identity served to at least partially isolate societies from some of the wilder excesses of the financial and corporate world in the early part of the century and the inter-war period. By focusing building society lending on property, primarily housing, it provided for their growth and stability. This also provided for their unique role as the major source of funding for the massive expansion of owner-occupation after the first world war.

As the government's Chief Registrar of Friendly Societies observed on the 1974 centenary of the 1874 Act, it 'provided the legal framework within the broad framework of which building societies have operated ever since' – or up to 1986 at least. The 1874 Act, as already noted, proved very durable. The development of the societies was by no means smooth. There were supplementary Acts, usually in response to some particular crisis which threatened confidence in 'the movement' (as it continued to be called). There was consolidating legislation in 1962. But the original framework proved adequate in broad terms as a basis for the massive modern expansion of the societies – in part because the societies remained, despite this massive growth, relatively simple institutions. They took in funds from investors largely in the form of personal savings. Much of this money was then loaned out long term to individual house buyers. The remainder was invested in a range of relatively secure public sector stock, providing a cushion of more liquid assets.

Initially, building societies as a financial sector were slow to expand and there were setbacks early on. In 1892, the massive Liberator building society collapsed. Like others at the time, it had loaned heavily to industrial and property companies. Its demise shook confidence in the movement as a whole. This was not helped by the subsequent collapse in 1911 of the Birkbeck, which had invested heavily in gilt-edged stocks that lost their shine as values tumbled.

By 1919 then, societies still represented relatively minor players on the national financial scene, but the game-plan had been drawn up. In 1919, less than one household in ten was owner-occupied – 80 per cent rented from private landlords. By 1990, 66 per cent of households were home owners. The massive growth of building societies, starting in the inter-war years, was a key factor, inextricably linked with the revolution in housing tenure over 70 years. It was linked not only economically, but politically, for the societies allied themselves closely with the interests of home owners and the expansion of home ownership as a form of tenure.

Significantly in this respect, the societies funded not only the purchase of new housing but also transfers of private rented and, more recently, public rented housing into owner-occupation.

The first real boom in private building came in the early 1930s. Ramsay MacDonald's Tory-dominated National government abolished subsidies to local authority housing built to meet general needs. During this period, real incomes of those in work were actually rising, encouraging house purchase and investment. The societies experienced a massive inflow of funds, since they offered security, liquidity and high returns compared to stocks and shares.

House prices, meanwhile, were static or falling in real terms. The result was a major upsurge in private building, primarily for owner-occupation, from around 130,000 in 1931 to an annual average of 260,000 over the period 1935 to 1939. Meanwhile, building society funds grew from £87 million in 1920 to £756 million by 1940.

With massive funds to lend, competition between societies grew, and lending practices changed in an attempt to encourage borrowing. Mortgage terms were extended from 15 to 20 years to the now customary 25, or even 30, years. The current practice of lending beyond the usual 70 to 75 per cent of house values, with the 'excess' being covered by an insurance policy, dates from this period.

Inter-society competition at this time generated increasing problems. One particular scheme involved lending beyond 70 to 75 per cent of valuation on the basis of deposits from builders, keen to secure loans for those buying their particular houses. This 'builders' pool' system, which became widespread in the 1930s, compounded the problems of downmarket lending on poorer quality housing, as builders sought to cash in on the housing boom.

The famous case of *Bradford third equitable building society v Borders* focused attention on deteriorating building standards and the questionable character of the builders' pool. Mrs Borders, whose new house had been particularly badly built, was taken to court by the society for non-payment. She brought counter-claims, which among other things questioned the legality of the builders' pool system. There were more widespread 'mortgage strikes', with several thousand people withholding mortgage payments, until the legality of the pool system was clarified or housing defects were corrected. The response was the 1939 Building Societies Act, which defined what represented acceptable security for loans.

After the second world war, societies continued to expand. Yet it was the revisiting of the earlier 'building society or bank' debate in the mid-1980s, and the accompanying deregulation of the financial markets, that saw new questions asked. The decisions made then were to have a massive impact over the next decade. ∎

Martin Boddy is director of the Centre for Urban Studies at the School for Policy Studies, University of Bristol

chapter 7

The origins of council housing

Peter Kemp

Was council housing developed as a response to the failures of the private market, or did the market fail because of state interference?

Most accounts of the origins of council housing see the 1919 Housing and Town Planning Act as the key milestone. This Act was significant because it introduced government subsidies for council housebuilding. It was also the first to place a duty on local authorities to survey the housing needs of their districts and to submit plans for the provision of houses to remedy shortages.

Although a handful of local authorities had begun to build unsubsidised rented housing towards the end of the 19th century, by 1914 only about 24,000 dwellings had been constructed, mostly by the large city councils. But immediately after the first world war, the government exhorted local authorities to build as many 'homes fit for heroes' as they could manage. By 1939, aided by government subsidy, they had built a million homes, accounting for ten per cent of the total stock. Councils had become firmly established as housing providers.

The 1919 Act was certainly an important turning point in the history of council housing. But why did this change of direction occur? As with so many other areas of our history, this is under dispute. But this is not simply a matter of academic pedantry. The conclusions one can draw are highly relevant to current debates about who should provide rented housing.

Some historians have seen the origins of council housing in the Victorian public health reform 'movement', believing it to be a natural and logical progression from early legislation on sanitation, building

Built to Last?

Scenic streets: the London county council's three-room Sylva Cottages, 1890

standards, overcrowding and slum clearance. Council housing was thus one more step to a more enlightened and humane social policy – a product of the growing awareness of bad housing conditions and, ultimately, a recognition of the need to provide decent, subsidised housing to rent for the poor. From this perspective, local authorities were the obvious candidates for the task of providing housing, since they were already responsible for public health and building regulations.

This interpretation of history usually focuses on major Acts of Parliament and on key individuals (usually male, often wealthy), whose foresight and humanity allowed them to be prime movers behind legislation for the benefit of the poor. Such laws are often referred to by the names of these 'great men'. For example, the 1919 Act is often called the Addison Act, after the minister responsible for piloting it through Parliament.

In recent years, this somewhat naive view of the inevitability of subsidised council housing has been challenged. A different approach focuses less on the good deeds of key individuals, more on social forces and conflicts. Instead of being regarded as passive recipients, ordinary men and women are often seen as having played a pivotal role. From this perspective, it is argued that there was nothing inevitable about the introduction of government subsidies for council housing – rather that it needs to be explained and not simply assumed.

So, at the risk of over-simplification, there are two competing explanations of the origins of subsidised council housing, each with its own variations, qualifications and subtleties. The first sees council housing as a response to the failure of the private market. The other says the market failed *because* of state interference – and that, far from being a solution, council housing was part of the problem.

The first view sees the introduction of subsidised council housing as a response to the failure of private landlords to provide decent quality housing at rents that working people could afford. Some authors focus on the long-term failure of the private landlord, while others also argue that there was a permanent, structural, pre-war collapse of investment in private housing to rent which forced the state to intervene in housing provision.

Prior to 1914, perhaps 90 per cent of housing was provided by private landlords, while rents were set by the interaction of supply and demand. Many poor people lived in appalling slum conditions, largely because that was all they could afford. While the introduction of minimum building standards and public health legislation did improve the quality of new construction, it also raised building costs and hence rents. Essentially, the problem was that many people's incomes were simply too low for them to afford decent housing.

It was to show that private enterprise really could provide decent housing at affordable rents that the 'model dwelling companies' were set up in the late 19th century. These forerunners of the housing association movement, such as Peabody and Guinness, constructed blocks of dwellings and aimed to give a five per cent return to their investors, compared with the eight per cent often secured on rented housing at that time. Yet their rents were usually still too high for the poorest households, and the dwellings were often let to the better-off working class.

This was also true of the (unsubsidised) housing built by local authorities before 1914. It was generally beyond the means of the poorest households. And, like the model dwelling companies' housing, it was often aimed at those considered to be the 'deserving poor', not those whom we would now regard as being most in need. Prior to 1914, a debate did emerge about whether local authorities should get more involved in providing rented housing. But even many of those in favour of subsidies for council housing saw local authorities as taking second place to the private sector, perhaps filling gaps in provision and providing a model with which the market could compete.

Some in the 'market failure' camp claim that there was a collapse of investment in rented housing before 1914, which signalled an end to private landlordism. The introduction of subsidies for council housing was a necessary consequence of this crisis, they say. From this point of view, the war merely influenced the timing of the introduction of subsidies, while rent controls were only another nail in the private landlord's coffin rather than the fatal blow.

An alternative explanation sees council housing as a consequence of the first world war. This view sees the pre-war slump of investment in rented housing construction as a cyclical downturn rather than permanent collapse – one from which it would have recovered had it not been for the introduction of rent controls in 1915 following rent strikes in Glasgow and elsewhere.

The introduction of central government subsidies in 1919 is seen by this camp as a direct consequence of rent controls. Politically, the housing shortage made it imperative that building took place after the war, yet it also made it impossible to remove rent controls. Unless rent controls were removed, private landlords would not build any houses, especially as building costs and interest rates had increased greatly during the war. Hence an emergency programme of subsidised council housebuilding had to be introduced to remove the shortage – thus making it possible to end rent controls and get the building of housing to rent back onto a commercial footing.

The subsequent failure to decontrol rents meant that private investment in rented housing never returned and council housing has remained with us ever since. For some, this transformation amounted to the 'sacrifice' of the private landlord, representing (for those on the left) a notable victory for working-class struggle or (for those on the right) a lack of political will to implement deregulation.

In trying to make sense of these competing views of housing history, it is helpful to distinguish between two separate (though related) questions. First, why did the government introduce housing subsidies in 1919 when previously it had been most reluctant to do so?

Second, why were local authorities given the subsidies and entrusted with responsibility for the housing programme? In other countries subsidies were focused on private landlords and housing associations, while municipal housing was given a relatively minor role.

Separating these issues makes it easier to understand why subsidies were introduced. The failure of the private sector to provide decent quality housing for the poorest households created growing pressures on government to do something about the housing question. The pre-war decade did see a major, though not a complete, collapse of investment in rented housing. This made some kind of state intervention very likely. Indeed, there is evidence to suggest that the war may have delayed the introduction of government subsidies. Even so, we do not know for sure what the precise nature and scale of the subsidy would eventually have been.

In the event, the war transformed the whole way housing was debated. The severe housing shortage that developed during the war and the social unrest this threatened made it urgent for the state to deal with it when war ended. The short-term increase in building costs and interest rates meant that, unaided, the private sector could not be relied upon to meet the shortage. Some kind of subsidy, therefore, was even more necessary to ensure that building took place in the immediate post-war period than it had been before 1914.

Secondly, the war had a significant effect upon the way assistance was provided. Consequently, local authorities emerged as the obvious candidates to carry out the post-war building programme. The wartime rent strikes (see chapter five) and profiteering by some private landlords meant that, politically, it was not possible to give subsidies to private landlords. Though never popular, they became widely reviled during and after the war, and this effectively precluded them from receiving state handouts. However, an additional Housing Act passed towards the end of 1919 did provide grants to private house builders.

Housing associations (or 'public utility societies' as they were known) were considered for the job of meeting the post-war housing shortage, but were not felt able to cope with the scale of the problem. Even so, the Addison Act of 1919 did make subsidies available to them on a similar basis to local authority building. The societies eventually constructed 4,545 dwellings under the Act, compared with 170,000 by local authorities, in England and Wales.

It was also considered whether central government itself should carry out the programme, but this course was rejected because the Ministry of Works did not have the necessary local knowledge. Local authorities did have knowledge of local housing market conditions, land supply and building costs. And unlike the public utility societies they collectively covered the whole country. Moreover, local councils already had building and other housing powers under pre-war legislation and hence some relevant experience. State housing was a demand of several groups representing working people at this time, while a number of official reports – including the Royal Commission on Scottish Housing, which was set up before the war but reported in 1917 – recommended that subsidies for municipal housing be introduced.

Yet many local authorities were initially reluctant to get involved in providing housing, especially if it meant a charge on the rates. This was partly why the 1919 Act subsidy was so generous. All their deficits above the product of a penny rate (four-fifths of a penny in Scotland) were met by the government. Despite this open-ended subsidy, rents charged on 1919 Act houses were still too high for many working-class tenants, and they were often let to better-off and lower middle-class households. Some councils even had to advertise their larger houses outside of the district in order to find tenants for them.

During 1919-20, the Ministry of Health urged authorities to build as many houses as they could. It gave advice on design as well as construction materials and methods, to hasten the implementation of the programme. Yet in 1921, the subsidies were prematurely axed. This is used by one commentator, Mark Swenarton, to justify his argument that the 'homes fit for heroes' campaign was designed as an insurance against revolution, aimed at buying off social unrest. Once the threat of revolution had receded, the insurance policy was no longer needed and could be terminated, especially in view of its high cost.

Cabinet minutes show that fear of revolution was certainly a significant factor behind the post-war housing programme, but Swenarton's case is too crude. It does not explain why subsidies were re-introduced (for private and municipal housebuilding) by the Conservatives in 1923. This was due to the growing housing shortage and the failure of the private sector to build many houses. The Labour government which briefly came to power in 1924 also introduced a subsidy – for municipal and private rented construction – which resulted in half a million council houses being built, compared with 75,000 under the less generous 1923 Act.

When the Conservatives returned to power in late 1924, they retained Labour's subsidy along with their own of 1923. While their legislation gave council housing only a residual role, Labour's 1924 Act directed councils to meet general needs. The Conservatives were 'reluctant collectivists' who supported this tenure largely because investment in privately rented construction had dried up and alternatives had to be found, while Labour favoured municipal provision.

It was the 1924 Act, rather than that of 1919, which really established council housing as a long-term feature of the housing market. It had little to do with slogans about homes for heroes, however, and instead reflected the collapse of private rental construction. Criticised in a Commons debate for interfering with private housing investment, Labour's minister of health, John Wheatley, pointed out that there was no investment in working-class homes. 'Are we to remain without houses,' he replied, 'merely because people who have money...refuse to invest that money directly in working-class houses?'

Some would say the lack of investment in private rented building after the war was due to the failure to decontrol rents. But rent control applied only to pre-1919 dwellings, not to new buildings. Other factors were more important, especially the dramatic increase in building costs at the end of the war and the (correct) expectation that they would eventually fall. Hence investing in rented housing would have meant making a capital loss when house prices eventually fell.

In the 1930s, when housing market conditions had improved, a revival of building for private rental (averaging over 66,000 units a year in 1933-39) did occur. But by then council housing and owner-occupation had become established as powerful competitors to the private landlord. And that they remain. ■

Peter Kemp is director of the ESRC Centre for Housing Research and Urban Studies at the University of Glasgow

chapter 8

Housing subsidies

Peter Malpass

Compared to the current complex rules on finance for council housing, most subsidy systems in operation since 1919 were models of simplicity

For more than 70 years, successive British governments have been drawn into repeated bouts of legislation on council house subsidies. The 1989 Local Government and Housing Act may have been the Conservatives' second attempt to reform the system after taking power in 1979, but it represented the 19th housing subsidies Act since 1919.

The frequency of legislation on housing subsidies in the council sector is not just a reflection of party differences. It has been produced by the sheer difficulty of finding a system that was effective in achieving central government objectives, without removing the cherished freedom of local authorities to control their own housing budgets, and especially their right to set rents. In pursuit of a robust and durable solution, complexity has increasingly driven out the simplicity of earlier subsidy systems.

By comparison with the 1989 Act, the majority of subsidy systems operated since 1919 were models of simplicity.

The first housing subsidy category can be described as investment subsidy, where the local authority was given a fixed cash sum, per dwelling, per year, for a specified period of years. The term *investment* subsidy is used because the subsidy was related to an authority's investment in new building, and represented a contribution towards loan charges arising from that new building.

The second category is *deficit* subsidy, which is based on the overall balance between income and expenditure in the housing revenue account (HRA).

The third category is *rent rebate* subsidy, and is different in certain important respects from the first two, mainly because it is calculated according to the incomes of individual tenants and because it can exist alongside both investment and deficit subsidy.

Historically, large-scale investment in council housing was launched in 1919 on the basis of a deficit subsidy system, which was very soon abandoned in favour of a succession of investment subsidy systems over the following 50 years.

It is only since 1972 that governments have returned to versions of deficit subsidy, and only in this period, too, that they have provided an explicit rent rebate subsidy. This prompts questions about why deficit subsidy was first adopted, only to be abandoned, and why the principle has been revived in recent times.

At the end of the first world war, building costs were very high, and rents could not cover expenditure on loan charges, as well as management and maintenance. Under the 1919 Act, the local authorities' liability to contribute to income deficits was limited to the product of a penny rate, and the exchequer made up the rest. This arrangement suited the local authorities, but left the exchequer exposed to an open-ended liability, a situation which highlights a basic feature of deficit subsidy systems: who decides the size of the deficit?

Central government was naturally inclined to be suspicious that local authorities would adopt extravagant building standards, but would set low rents. Even where authorities set modest standards, the system put no pressure on them to be efficient and scrupulous about containing costs.

In practice, the Ministry of Health set up an elaborate administrative apparatus, based on 11 regional offices, designed to monitor and control local authority behaviour. Where rents were deemed to be too low, subsidy could be withheld, subject to appeal to a tribunal. The city of Bristol, for instance, was faced with loss of subsidy after deciding in 1920 to reduce rents because they were beyond the reach of many families on the waiting list.[1] Eventually the tribunal ruled in the city's favour and the subsidy was paid, but this illustration shows how deficit subsidy systems complicate the relationship between central and local government. The essential point is that, although local authorities incur the costs and set the rents,

Flat out: with so many tenants dependent on housing benefit, the current system of annual rent increases above inflation has huge implications for public expenditure and work incentives. Reform of housing benefit has to be a priority for any government serious about welfare reform

Nick Dawe

central government covers the deficit and therefore has a close interest in the relationship between income and expenditure.

Central government escaped from the complexities of deficit subsidy by adopting the investment subsidy model in 1923. The 1923 Housing Act said that in future new building by local authorities would attract a subsidy of £6 per dwelling, per year, for 20 years.

The Labour government of 1924 introduced a higher rate of exchequer subsidy, payable over a longer period, and in view of recent central government attitudes to subsidy and to new housebuilding by councils, it is interesting to note the nature of the bargaining over the subsidy level at that time. The government wanted houses to be built, and the authorities were in a strong position to negotiate subsidy.

The Labour minister of health, John Wheatley, reported to the House of Commons that the local authorities had pressed for £12 per house and that: 'It was only at the very last moment, by a very strong appeal to the local authorities, that they agreed to accept £9.'[2]

The 1924 Act reintroduced the notion of a mandatory rate fund contribution (RFC), and this remained a feature of all subsequent Acts until 1956. In addition, authorities were permitted to make discretionary RFCs and were *required* to make an RFC to balance the account if there remained a deficit at the end of the financial year.

Thus, the open-ended responsibility for dealing with deficits lay at the local level throughout the period from 1923 to 1972. They could choose to remove deficits by either raising rents or making an RFC, but the requirement was that – one way or another – the HRA should balance each year.

There were several features of the investment subsidy approach which enabled it to survive for so long. First, it proved to be an effective way of stimulating housing production, and sustained the growth of council housing during periods when policy favoured high output, in the 1950s and 1960s.

Secondly, it gave central government some leverage on the amount and type of new building; the centre was able to raise or lower output according to the incentive provided by the value of subsidy, and it was able to influence the balance between building for general needs and slum clearance.

Thirdly, fixed annual subsidies appealed to the Treasury because they meant that its financial liability was capped and predictable each year.

Fourthly, the system gave local authorities considerable autonomy over such key aspects of housing policy as rents, management and maintenance (M&M) expenditure and the size of their capital programmes. Councils had an incentive to control costs, because increased costs would not be reflected in higher exchequer subsidy.

Fifthly, central government could influence local authority rents by means of financial leverage, but without formally breaching local autonomy in the matter. This became important from the mid-1950s, when the government adopted rent pooling as a device for levering rents upwards.

A product of the commitment to fixed annual subsidies was that successive systems were rather crude and insensitive to local cost variations. There were attempts in various Acts to differentiate subsidy levels according to urban or rural location, or, later, for high land costs, but the categories were widely drawn and the outcome was that subsidy was not closely related to local circumstances. Also, because authorities had control of capital investment for many years, there emerged a pattern of wide variation in loan charges, reflecting different rates of building at different times. This in turn influenced rents and levels of RFCs.

By the late 1960s, critics of prevailing policies on rents and subsidies were arguing that council rents generally were too low and that rent setting was approached from the wrong direction. The gradual spread of 'fair' rents in the private sector after the 1965 Rent Act began to change the long-standing pattern in which council rents had usually exceeded controlled private sector rents.

The fact that council subsidies were fixed cash amounts meant that rents tended to be set in terms of what was needed to bridge the gap between subsidy and expenditure, and this might bear little relation to what houses were actually worth, given the impact of inflation. Subsidies were also inequitably distributed amongst local authorities and their tenants.

The outcome of this sort of critique was a package of proposals based on fair rents (setting rents in accordance with current value), deficit subsidy and a separate rent rebate system. These proposals were, however, politically unacceptable to the Labour government in the late 1960s. Fair rents implied a complete removal of local autonomy in rent setting, and implied very large increases for some authorities. Deficit subsidy approaches permit negative subsidies, or HRA surpluses, in certain circumstances, and Labour opposed the idea of 'profits' from council housing.

The government therefore held out against reform, but it did begin another policy trend which has been highly significant in subsequent developments. Economic difficulties in 1967 led the government to cut back on the party's long-established commitment to high levels of council housebuilding, and in retrospect 1968 can be seen as marking the end of the high output phase of post-war British housing policy.

The Conservative government which took office in 1970 enthusiastically embraced both lower building rates and the reform of rents and subsidies policy. The 1972 Housing Finance Act was a mould-breaking event – it marked the end of 50 years of continuity around forms of investment subsidy. But it was a seriously flawed measure, both technically and politically (see chapter 15). The emphasis in the Act was on rents rather than subsidies, following the logic that rents should be set first so that need for subsidy could then be calculated. Local authorities were instructed to raise rents by annual instalments until fair rent levels were reached, but, unlike previous measures, the 1972 Act contained no financial measures to ensure that authorities did what they were told.

The 1970s represented a period of digression from, and reversion to, financial leverage on local authority rents. The 1972 Act was the digression, which was repealed in 1975 and replaced by a temporary measure, pending creation of a more permanent solution. But some important developments did take place at that time. In particular a broad consensus was established around the idea that council rents should reflect the current value of money rather than historic costs, and that there should be a separate rent rebate system to channel assistance to people in greatest need.

Another important development of the 1970s, implemented in the 1980s, was the notional housing revenue account as the basis for subsidy payments. The notional HRA combines elements of central control and local autonomy, and, like pre-1972 systems, relies on financial leverage as the means of applying central pressure on rents.

After the political difficulties encountered in the early 1970s, arising from attempts to instruct local authorities to raise rents, the 1980 Housing Act reverted to a system of setting subsidy first and letting councils make the subsequent rent decisions. The 1980 system was clearly influenced by the need to accommodate a degree of local autonomy in rent-setting, but at the same time it was a policy driven more by subsidy considerations than a concern about rent levels.

It is in the nature of deficit subsidy systems that the legislation specifies ways of calculating assistance rather than stating amounts of entitlement. But this inevitably clouds the situation for local authorities, who are left with no certainty about movements in subsidy from year to year.

The 1980 Act contained a formula for the calculation of subsidy, based on the amount paid in the previous year and notional changes in income and expenditure (principally income from rents and expenditure on management and maintenance). Each year the secretary of state issued two 'determinations', representing his assumptions about changes in rents and M&M expenditure. The amount of leverage on rents depended upon the size of the gap between these two determinations.

In practice, the secretary of state tended to assume that rents would rise faster than M&M expenditure, and most authorities experienced sharp cutbacks in subsidy, especially at first. In aggregate terms the amount of deficit subsidy fell by over 80 per cent in the first three years that the system was in operation and, by the late 1980s, four out of five authorities were no longer receiving Housing Act subsidy (but they were all receiving rent rebate subsidy).

The effect of the leverage approach to raising rents meant that rents could only be driven upwards by the centre if it was assumed that M&M expenditure rose more slowly than rent income, and therefore that increases in rent were reflected in lower subsidy rather than improved services to tenants. In this sense, the government became the agent of disrepair in the public sector.

Calculation of actual subsidy on the basis of a notional HRA was, then, a way of both capping exchequer liability for deficit subsidy and a way of keeping rents rising. It was also a way of shifting the balance between deficit and rebate subsidy, and the consequences of this aspect of the system finally led to its downfall. The 1980 Act system was designed for a period of stock *contraction* rather than growth, and for the new era of HRA surpluses, rather than deficits.

A system based on current value rents and deficit subsidy implies, especially in periods of price inflation and low investment, that deficits will disappear and surpluses will arise. The issues, then, are: who determines the size of surpluses, how are they made actual rather than notional, and who has the right to dispose of them?

A further problem arises with systems such as the 1980 Act in their approach to rent setting: central government pressure can only be put on rents by reducing the size of notional deficits, and once deficits disappear, authorities regain much greater autonomy.

The leverage approach adopted in 1980 can be seen as a direct response to the difficulties of *instructing* authorities to raise rents in 1972, and in their design, the architects of the 1980 system recognised the problem of dealing with surpluses. Essentially what they did was to design the method of calculating rate support grant (in the 1980 Local Government, Planning and Land Act) in such a way that authorities with *notional* HRA surpluses could be put under pressure to make those *actual* surpluses and to transfer them to the general rate fund.

In practice this mechanism was used only once, in 1981/82, and then abandoned because of political opposition from Conservative-controlled local authorities. The outcome was that well over a quarter of all authorities soon moved into surplus, thereby subsidising the rates.

The current financial regime was devised in the late 1980s to overcome what central government saw as unreasonably high levels of subsidy to council housing. On the one hand, it was paying rent rebate subsidy to more than 100 authorities where the HRA was actually in surplus, and, on the other hand, another group of authorities were seen to be 'indiscriminately' subsidising council housing through rate fund contributions.

The ring-fence around the HRA is designed to remove 'excess' rebate and subsidy and RFCs. The incorporation of rebate subsidy into the new HRA subsidy can be seen in terms of the government's need to give itself renewed leverage on rents, whilst preserving an element of local control over rents. The problem, however, is that the centre went beyond the ringfence and introduced new areas of complexity in the form of much more sophisticated approaches to assessing changes in rents and M&M expenditure.

The history of British council housing subsidy systems provides a way of explaining the complexity of the new regime. The current system is very much a product of its antecedents. For many years, subsidy policy was about giving incentives to build, and the *pattern* of building was perhaps less important to governments than the aggregate level of output.

The old subsidy systems were simple but crude, making very little allowance for local cost variations. However, they did allow for local autonomy and included the important safety valve of discretionary RFCs. Nevertheless, wide variations in costs of new development and the level of debt charges per dwelling generated significant variations in rents.

A major proportion of the difficulty now facing policymakers is due to the *laissez-faire* attitudes of the past. Not only were authorities free to set their own investment levels, but also their own administrative structures and accounting conventions.

In an inflationary environment, governments will naturally want to keep rents on the move, irrespective of ideological preferences for public or private housing. In the 1950s and 1960s, the rate of new building, and therefore the rate of debt expansion, made it possible to lever rents upwards by under-funding new building and relying on rent pooling to raise rents for all. But in the present period things are not so simple. With so many tenants now dependent on housing benefit, a simple strategy of annual rent increases above inflation has serious implications for public expenditure and work incentives. Reform of housing benefit had to be an urgent priority for the incoming Labour government. ∎

Notes

1. M Daunton (Ed), *Councillors and tenants: local authority housing in English cities 1919-1939*, Leicester University Press, 1984, pp.198-9
2. *House of Commons debates* Vol 175, col 102, June 1924

Peter Malpass is professor of housing policy at the University of the West of England in Bristol

chapter 9

Rents within reach

Peter Malpass

The argument about 'bricks and mortar' subsidies versus income subsidies for poorer tenants has its origins in the early days of rent rebate schemes

At the present time, 67 per cent of council tenants rely on housing benefit to help them pay their rent, and the idea of rent rebates to assist those on low incomes is a very well-established feature of housing policy in all rented sectors. But it was not always like this.

The provision of rebates on a large scale is a relatively modern development – as recently as 25 years ago less than 10 per cent of council tenants received rebates, and only since 1972 have local authorities been required to provide rebates for low-income tenants.

In fact, the origins of housing benefit lie in debates nearly 70 years ago about the proper way to distribute housing subsidy. The argument was over whether subsidies should reduce the standard rents for all houses, irrespective of the incomes of individual tenants, or be restricted to those tenants who qualified for help on grounds of low income. This came to be expressed as a debate about subsidies for 'bricks and mortar' or for 'people', but it is really about pricing policy and the relationship between housing and social security.

The idea of providing rent rebates emerged in the late 1920s, after a decade of housing subsidies which had been introduced to regenerate housebuilding after the first world war. In the immediate aftermath of the war, housing construction costs rose to several times their pre-war level, and, without subsidy, the rents of new houses would have been well beyond the reach of working-class families, even those on relatively high earnings.

Jon Walter

Poverty trap: today's benefit dependency has its roots in pre-war policies

Although costs fell away from their 1920 peak, the 1920s as a whole was still a decade of relatively high house prices and interest rates. In this context, it was accepted that assistance was appropriate, and subsidies were provided for private builders as well as local authorities.

However, towards the end of the decade, the situation began to look rather different and new arguments emerged. Prices were falling, which meant the possibility of a viable market for unsubsidised new private housing for the rather better-off workers. It was also becoming clear that a decade of housing subsidies had been of very little benefit to the least well-off; despite subsidies, rents in many areas had remained too high for council housing to be affordable by the poor.

By 1929, politicians were turning their attention to the problem of a century of virtually unregulated urban housing development for the industrial working class: the slums were once again on the political agenda, and it was recognised that any programme of slum clearance would involve the rehousing of large numbers of poor families.

The response of the Conservative government in the late 1920s was to encourage local authorities to take advantage of falling prices, and lower standards, in order to channel new houses to lower-income families at rents below those set for earlier houses. The Tories also went into the 1929 general election with a policy of 'reconditioning' the slums rather than demolishing them.

However, a minority Labour government was elected, and the new minister of health, Arthur Greenwood, brought forward a Bill designed to launch a national programme of slum clearance. The Bill contained proposals for a new subsidy, specifically related to the number of people rehoused from slum clearance. This was to exist alongside the 1924 Act subsidy for 'general needs housing'. The slum clearance subsidy was presented as more generous than the general needs subsidy, but the Bill contained no mechanisms to ensure that the recipients of this extra help were those who actually needed it.

Although the textbooks generally report that the 1930 Housing Act introduced rent rebates, it is important to note that it was not the policy of the Labour government at that time to encourage rebating. In fact, the freedom for local authorities to provide rent rebate schemes was introduced into the Bill at a late stage in its passage through parliament, and as a result of backbench pressure rather than government initiative. Both Labour and Conservative politicians in those days were generally opposed to the principle of rent rebates, albeit for different reasons.

Labour's opposition rested on its wider distaste for means-testing, while for the Tories the objection was that rebates in effect represented a subsidy to employers paying low wages.

The campaign for rent rebates was led by Eleanor Rathbone, who sat as an Independent MP for the English Universities between 1929 and 1946, supported by Sir Ernest Simon, Liberal member for Manchester Withington between 1929 and 1931.

Eleanor Rathbone's greatest achievement was her role in the establishment of family allowances in 1945. As early as 1924 she set up the Family Endowment Society to campaign for family allowances, and its influence was brought to bear in the cause of rent rebates too. In her early advocacy of rebates, Rathbone referred to them as 'children's rent rebates'. Her argument was that rent-paying capacity was related to the number of dependents in a family, hence the view that if subsidies were to be available in council housing, they should take account of different household circumstances.

In her maiden speech in the House of Commons, Rathbone went straight into an attack on general subsidy. 'It would have been far better if the local authorities had fixed the rents – I know I am enunciating a heresy in the view of most people here – at the economic value of the house, and had then used the subsidy according to principles clearly laid down and carefully thought out, to relieve the needs of those who most needed housing relief,' she said.[1]

In the debates on the 1930 Housing Bill, Eleanor Rathbone and Sir Ernest Simon argued their case in the face of official indifference and opposition. Simon himself described their battle in these words: 'Miss Rathbone and I fought hard during the various stages of the Greenwood Bill to secure an amendment to the effect that the subsidies should only be given to those who need them and only for so long as they need them; in other words, that the subsidy should be attached to the tenant and not to the house. Mr Greenwood resisted our amendments, but did ultimately accept amendments to the effect that, although the local authority was not compelled to confine the subsidy to those who need them, it was at least authorised to do so.'[2] This account is substantially corroborated by Eleanor Rathbone's biographers.[3]

Thus it was that the 1930 Housing Act gave a power for councils to grant rent rebates, on such terms and conditions as they thought fit. What was to become the major form of rent assistance half a century later actually began as a reluctant concession to a couple of troublesome backbenchers in 1930.

There was no compulsion on local authorities, there were no guidelines as to how rebate schemes might be designed and implemented, nor was the power to provide rebates extended beyond those dwellings built under the 1930 Act. It was clear from the way in which Greenwood referred to Labour's rents policy that the government did not envisage a rebating approach. He was still talking about using the new subsidy to provide some houses at lower rents, rather than rebates for specific *tenants*.

After the fall of the Labour government in 1931, the new national government, dominated by Conservatives, continued the lukewarm line on rebates. For the Tories, the preferred route to lower rents for the poor was still lower standards. However, the 1935 Housing Act introduced the requirement that local authorities should maintain a single housing revenue account for all their houses and flats, and this opened up the possibility of rent rebate schemes which were applicable across the whole stock.

It is hardly surprising in view of the attitude of successive governments in the 1930s that the local authorities on the whole made little use of their power to introduce rebate schemes. They had reasons of their own for not being enthusiastic about rebates. The provision of rebates implies a commitment to poor families, but local authorities generally seem to have been unwilling to give preference to such families.

This was pointed out by Simon in 1933 when he wrote that not only were the 1924 Act houses too expensive for the lower paid, but also local authorities had not gone out of their way to make these houses available to those in greatest need. 'Unfortunately, although the local authorities have generally passed resolutions in favour of housing large families, those who have administered the letting of the houses have tended to give the first chance to "good" tenants, that is to say, those with a fair income and few children.'[4]

Apart from their attitude to tenants, local authorities had other reasons for being wary of rent rebate schemes. Given the lack of advice and guidance from central government, local councils adopting the idea of rebating found themselves entering an uncharted area, full of administrative, financial and political difficulties. In addition to the complexity of a scheme which varied rents according to household composition and/or income, there was the problem of monitoring changes of circumstances and keeping the rents actually charged in line with such changes. All this meant an increased workload for the housing management staff.

However, perhaps of greater significance was the problem of designing a feasible scheme. Authorities had to use the exchequer subsidy, which was paid in the form of a fixed sum per house, per year, as a pool from which to pay needs-related rebates. This meant taking subsidy that was paid for one purpose and redistributing it for another. The subsidy pool was finite, although it could be topped up from local rates income, and the problem was to decide how much of that pool to allocate to rebates, and then to construct an income scale of need and a benefit scale which would fit together in such a way that the level of demand did not drain the pool too quickly. The penalty for miscalculation would be either a scheme which failed to provide adequate help for those in need, or which was so generous that funds ran out and ratepayers had to be asked to balance the account.

Then there was the opposition of tenants themselves. During the 1930s, rent rebate schemes proved to be highly unpopular with existing tenants, partly because of the redistribution of subsidy which was required. The use of housing subsidy as a rebates pool required that the benefit of subsidy had to be reduced or withheld altogether from the more affluent tenants.

To introduce a rebate scheme into an existing stock of houses therefore required rent *increases* for some at the same time as reductions for others. The better-off tenants were thus being asked, in a sense, to subsidise the reduced rents of their poorer neighbours. It is easy to see that this could generate considerable resentment amongst the better-off, with the threat of political unpopularity and even electoral defeat for the councillors responsible.

It is important to remember that in the 1920s it had been necessary for tenants to show that they earned enough to afford the rent of a new council house. But in the rather different climate of the 1930s their affluence was turned against them; the London county council actually wrote to 300 tenants on two estates in 1934 suggesting that they no longer needed subsidised housing and should leave. It must have seemed very unfair to these people, who had been selected precisely because they were deemed to be able to pay the rent for a new council house, now to find that they were expected to give up their home for tenants who could not afford the full rent.

Attempts to persuade better-off tenants to leave were in fact rare, but raising their rents in order to give rebates to the poor must have spurred some to opt for alternatives, such as home ownership, which experienced a boom in the mid-1930s. Council housing had acquired a rather privileged status in the early post-war years, accommodating the better-off skilled workers and the self-consciously respectable working class. Rent rebate schemes represented a threat to their position, not just because of the increase in rent but because of the accompanying influx of the less well-off and less respectable elements of the working class. Council housing in the 1930s was under attack; on the one hand there was the criticism that affluence was being unjustly subsidised, while on the other hand the extension of subsidy to the poor led to allegations of 'coals in the bath' behaviour by the 'undeserving' poor who did not know how to live in decent housing.

In practice most local authorities avoided any entanglement with rent rebates, and even the recently formed Central Housing Advisory Committee in the first report of its housing management committee in 1939 expressly avoided discussion of what it called the 'controversial question' of rebates. This report stated that only 80 local authorities (out of over 1,400) operated formal rent rebate schemes, although others were prepared to give rebates on merit.

In Scotland, the Department of Health pursued a rather more enthusiastic line than the Ministry of Health in England and Wales, and there was more local interest north of the border.

Those few authorities that did introduce rebate schemes tended to confine them to tenants rehoused from slum clearance areas under the 1930 Housing Act. Despite the small number of schemes, the variety was immense. At one extreme was the Middlesbrough scheme of 'rent differentiation', which attempted to grade houses and tenants in such a way that 'grade A' houses (nearest the shops and private residential areas) were let at the full economic rent to the highest-paid tenants, while 'grade C' houses were allocated to the poor at low rents.

At the opposite extreme was the Leeds scheme which incorporated the entire housing stock (except the 1919 Act houses which were excluded for legal reasons). This scheme involved distributing subsidy in such a way that large families on low incomes could qualify for a 'nil rent' assessment. Most other schemes involved setting a standard rent as the starting point for rebates, and they often included a minimum charge beyond which no rebate could be provided however low the tenant's income.

The experience of Leeds city council probably acted as a warning to many other authorities and it is worth expanding a little on what happened there. In April 1934 the Labour-controlled council introduced a scheme in which all subsidy was drawn into the rent rebate pool, and full economic rents were set for all houses. This meant increases on the basic rent of between 70 and 100 per cent, before calculation of rebates according to family income and needs. The rebates resulted in some tenants paying no rent at all, while others on higher incomes paid a proportion of the full rent and some received no rebate. Thus there was a group of tenants who were much worse off as a result of the scheme's generosity to others.

The political risks were obvious: 'Given the social composition of council estates in the early 1930s, before slum clearance was in full swing, it was inevitable that a scheme which provided for certain tenants to live rent free, and in effect extended a means test to households not applying for public assistance but merely seeking to avoid higher rents, would alienate both the tenants and public opinion in general.'[5]

The rent rebate scheme was bitterly opposed by tenants and there were threats of rent strikes, but in the end the tenants' association fought the issue through the courts, and lost. However, it was also opposed through the ballot box and was held to be a major factor in Labour's defeat in the 1935 municipal elections.

Another example of the bitterness generated by rent rebate schemes in the 1930s was the proposal by the Conservative-controlled Birmingham city council in 1939. This was an attempt to drive better-off tenants out of council housing and to remove similar applicants from the waiting list in order that the city could proceed with meeting the enormous need arising from slum clearance. Again it was the introduction of a means test which aroused most opposition, but in this case there was a prolonged rent strike by over 7,000 tenants. The approach of the second world war overshadowed these events and when the war started the rebate plan was dropped.[6]

By the end of the 1930s the idea of rent rebates was looking like a failed experiment – unpopular with governments, local authorities and tenants alike. It remained a very marginal feature of local authority housing provision, in terms of the number of schemes, the proportion of tenants in any area who benefited and the amount of subsidy diverted into the rebate pool. Underlying the debate about rebating was confusion over the distinction between housing subsidy, which is paid as part of a general pricing policy, and income-related assistance, which is part of social security policy. Housing subsidy implicitly reflects the view that *landlords* should be paid a form of compensation in order to reduce prices below what they would otherwise be. A rebate is in effect a payment to tenants to enable them to afford the rent set by the landlord.

This latter point is more easily grasped in relation to the private rented sector, where it is clearly understood that landlords set rents in accordance with the market value of their properties, rather than the circumstances of individual tenants. The purpose of housing benefit is to ensure that those tenants can afford the rent set by the landlord, and therefore it is clearly the case that tailoring rents to individual tenants' needs is not a landlord activity.

In the context of the 1930s, the debate was set up solely in terms of the distribution of housing subsidy, and the confusion has continued to affect council housing for the last 60 years. After the second world war rebating went into decline for a decade, and it was not until 25 years after the 1930 Act that governments began to encourage authorities to develop rent rebate schemes.

From 1955 until 1972 this took the form of urging authorities to redistribute their general housing subsidy in the shape of income-related rebates. It was not until the 1972 Housing Finance Act that a specific rent rebate subsidy was introduced, but this still left local housing authorities with partial responsibility for a form of social security, and there then emerged the so-called 'better-off problem'. Many tenants were entitled to either a rent rebate or supplementary benefit, but it was sometimes difficult to tell which was the right choice.

The introduction of housing benefit in 1982 went some way towards eliminating that problem, and it represented a further major rationalisation in the sense that housing benefit was at last recognised as a form of social security, and responsibility for it in central government was transferred from the DoE (now DETR) to the DHSS (now DSS). Unfortunately, this logic was not applied at the local level and local authorities remained responsible for housing benefit administration.

The latest twist in the saga is that from April 1990, the so-called new regime for local authority housing finance once again blurred the distinction between housing subsidy and income maintenance. Provision for rent rebates was subsumed within the new housing revenue account subsidy, thereby raising again old arguments about better-off tenants subsidising their poorer neighbours – only this time local authorities had freedom to ignore central government policy. ■

Notes

1. *House of Commons debates* Vol 230, col 973, July 1929

2. Sir E Simon, *The anti-slum campaign*, Longmans, Green & Co, 1933, p.40

3. M Stocks, *Eleanor Rathbone*, Gollancz, 1949, p.146

4. Sir E Simon, *op.cit.*, p.24

5. R Finnegan, 'Housing policy in Leeds between the wars', in J Melling (ed), *Housing, social policy and the state*, Croom Helm, 1981

6. S Schifferes, 'Council tenants and housing policy in the 1930s', in *Housing and class in Britain*, Political Economy of Housing Workshop, 1976

Peter Malpass is professor of housing policy at the University of the West of England in Bristol

chapter 10

A prefab future

Martin Pawley

In the aftermath of the second world war, housing shortages meant that bombers gave way to houses on the nation's production lines

Because the appreciating house has for so long been the main plank in the middle class black economy, it is difficult to remember what it was like when flats and houses were simply consumer goods like telephones or motor cars. Yet, only 40 years ago, that is what they were. Politicians, builders and householders all thought of housing as a product.

At the end of the second world war the vast majority of people in Britain rented their homes, and expected to go on doing so all their lives. They rented them on terms which were actually less arduous than those enjoyed by the drivers of company cars today. It is interesting to remember this when people argue that ownership is a 'privileged' or 'democratic' form of tenure, while rental is 'oppressive' or 'feudal'.

Today, when 68 per cent of households in the country are owner-occupiers, more than half the new car registrations are 'feudal' corporate perks. And the same people who would consider themselves to be in a state of 'feudal' servitude if they had not bought their own home, would also consider it 'oppressive' to have to buy their own car.

There is no good reason why all houses should appreciate like antique furniture. They could be as plentiful as cardboard boxes: they could be produced and sold like cars. The drivers of the shiny new saloons that roar off the forecourts each year do not own them: they 'rent' them on terms as oppressive as those endured by the frank-tenementers and free-socagers of medieval times, and yet they consider themselves a privileged motoring class.

Fast talking: a 1945 Labour election poster makes house building a clear priority

This is a paradox that illuminates the way in which the consideration of any alternative to the sale and resale of expensive handmade houses has disappeared from the political agenda in recent years. Crowded out by massive mortgage-peddling, alternatives have only recently, with the crisis of homelessness, begun to stir again.

The idea of mass-producing houses to conquer the problems of homelessness and overcrowding dates from the aftermath of the first world war, but prefabrication has a much longer history, stretching back long before Henry Ford began mass-producing cars in 1913. William the Conqueror's army brought prefabricated forts to England in 1066, and transportable barracks and hospitals were shipped to the Crimea in 1854.

In the aftermath of the first world war 74 years later, nearly 30,000 steel and concrete prefabricated houses were built in Britain because of the housing shortage and the scarcity of skilled building labour. But these houses were not intended as short-life, replaceable units. The Swiss architect Le Corbusier wrote in 1923: 'Most ordinary people equate getting a house with writing their will.' This misconception was to dog the prefabrication of houses right up until recent times.

Everywhere, except in the United States, inter-war experiments in prefabrication took the form of heavy concrete or steel structures. Inevitably there were problems of cracking, leaking and corrosion and, because of the political and economic turbulence of the era, these problems were never solved by continuous technical development. In fact, the same prefabrication methods were to re-appear – along with the same problems – in the 1960s when heavy concrete system building enjoyed its last boom.

True mass production of houses began in America, the first country to motorise, and the first to become hypnotised by the promise of the production line. There, the average cost of a house had increased by 200 per cent between 1913 and 1926, while the average cost of a car fell by 50 per cent. Several individuals grasped the implications of this.

The first glimpse of a truly mass-produced prefabricated home came in 1927 when Richard Buckminster Fuller, an inventor who had served in the US Navy during the first world war, patented a mast-supported prefabricated light alloy house that was air-deliverable – by airship. But Fuller was never able to put this house into production.

More conventional-looking production line dwellings were first onto the market. With the advent of the New Deal in 1933, special task forces like the Tennessee Valley Authority and the Farm Security Administration financed the development of light, timber-frame truckable dwellings that were produced in large numbers.

But the real boom in lightweight, short-life prefabrication came with the entry of the United States into the second world war, when the needs of war production led to the rehousing of more than nine million workers and their families in less than three years. During this time, architects like Walter Gropius and Konrad Wachsmann, and inventors like Fuller, exploited lightness and expendability in successful mass production.

Post-war plans for making good the United States housing deficit involved the emergence of a massive prefabrication industry based on automotive and aviation technology. Bombers were to give way to houses on the production lines and aviation engineers planned their entry into the housing market.

During the war, British fact-finding teams went to the United States to study the creation of the new war-production towns by prefabrication. By 1944 in Britain, it was clear that the loss of 750,000 houses from bombing, the effects of rent control upon private landlords, four years of non-building and the imminent demobilisation of six million conscripted servicemen had created a massive post-war housing crisis that would erupt the moment the war ended. Successive wartime government committees considered the crisis, and their reports concluded that a state housing programme was the only answer.

This was a bipartisan conclusion. Modest building society proposals for a housing association-administered programme of private rental housing were rejected in favour of 'new technology'. Just as in America Curtiss Wright aircraft engineers were ready to plough their redundancy pay into 'housing factories', so in Britain the government was paying for the design of prefabricated houses to be assembled on the production lines that manufactured Spitfires, Lancasters and military trucks.

It was Winston Churchill, the Tory prime minister of the wartime coalition government, who first announced the emergency factory-made (EFM) housing programme. In March 1944, he announced a Ministry of Works emergency project to build 500,000 'new technology' prefabricated temporary houses directly the war ended. 'The emergency programme is to be treated as a military evolution handled by the government with private industry harnessed in its service', said Churchill. 'As much thought will go into the prefabricated housing programme as went into the invasion of Africa.'

In the event, military planning proved less successful in dealing with post-war economics than it had in dealing with the enemy. The design of the Ministry of Works temporary houses owed its origins to a number of wartime studies carried out by the motor and aircraft industries. The first prototype to be unveiled was the motor industry contribution, a steel panelled 'experimental temporary bungalow' called the 'Portal' after the minister of works, Lord Portal.

With a floor area of 616 square feet – one third larger than the minimum size laid down by the 1919 Tudor Walters report on space standards in public housing – and an estimated cost of £675 fully furnished, including fitted bathroom, kitchen and refrigerator, the proposed rent for the Portal was to be ten shillings (50p) a week for a life of ten years.

The next house was the 'Arcon', an asbestos-clad variant of the Portal, with the same prefabricated kitchen and bathroom capsule. Then came the most sophisticated of an eventual total of no less than 1,400 proposed designs. The 'AIROH' house (Aircraft Industries Research Organisation on Housing) was a 675 square foot, 10-tonne all-aluminium bungalow assembled from four sections, each delivered to the site on a lorry, fully furnished right down to the curtains. The four house sections were linked, using the same type of bolted connection as aircraft wing root joints. The proposed rate of production of complete houses was to be an incredible one every 12 minutes. This was possible because the completely equipped and furnished AIROH could be assembled from only 2,000 components, while the aircraft it would replace on the production line required 20,000.

In retrospect, it is clear that the EFM programme was the nucleus of what might have developed into a 'new technology' housing industry. Plans were made to use surplus airfield construction plant for site preparation, and records were set for speed of erection before the war ended. In April 1945, an Arcon house was completed and handed over to its new occupants by 22 men in under eight hours. In May an AIROH was erected on a bombed site in London's Oxford Street in just four hours.

But the EFM programme was not without its enemies. Even before the end of the war, the second reading of the Housing (Temporary Accommodation) Bill, which moved the allocation of £150 million for the production of prefabs, was refused by members who, like many people outside parliament, had come to believe that the Portal, the Arcon and the AIROH were intended to be the permanent houses of the future.

How far the alarm of the construction industry and the banks and building societies contributed to this myth has never been determined, but the state-funded construction of half a million prefabricated dwellings to be assembled by non-construction industry labour and let at controlled rents cannot have been a matter of indifference to the organisations that had dominated the housing market for so long. The establishment of a successful prefabricated housing industry based on automotive and aviation technology would have transformed, perhaps for ever, the balance that had historically existed between the scarce stock of existing housing and the rate of new construction.

In the United States, where the prefabrication boom of the war years left a well-established mobile home industry behind it, annual prefabricated short-life housing completions rose from 37,000 in 1946 to over 500,000 by the early 1970s. The existence of such an alternative source of housing in Britain would certainly, and repeatedly, have eased the problem of the homeless ever since.

In March 1945, the coalition government published a white paper on housing policy, in which the first two years after the war were designated 'emergency production years'. During this time the EFMs were to play a vital part, with the first 150,000 allocated to local authorities to meet emergency housing need. By this time, rising labour and material costs, as well as some refinement of their design, had increased the projected cost of all the EFMs, notably the Portal, which had been re-engineered so that it sat flat on the ground instead of being raised some six inches above it.

This meant that the unit cost for all EFMs had risen to between £800 and £1,400 – between ten and 30 per cent more than the cost of a conventional house. The programme remained intact because of its promised speed, but its future was now precarious.

Clement Attlee's Labour party, which won the general election of July 1945 with a large majority, inherited the EFM programme when it took office and presided over the last act in the drama. Another housing white paper, published in August, confessed that the Portal had been abandoned for lack of steel and announced yet more cost increases for the Arcon and AIROH. Nonetheless the new minister of health (then responsible for housing) announced in October 1945 that the programme would proceed together with conventional house construction and an aggressive policy of municipalisation for privately rented stock. By 1946, the ministry was issuing six housing directives a week. But in the event, the EFM programme contributed little to the total of 1.2 million new homes built between 1945 and 1950.

Production of the major types of EFM for local authorities continued until 1947, but only 170,000 of the 500,000 units Winston Churchill had spoken of were completed before the dollar convertibility crisis put a stop to the programme altogether. Of these, the largest number (54,000) were AIROH houses, and 46,000 were Arcon. The rest were made up of smaller numbers of different designs.

By chance, one of the AIROH houses went to the mother and father of Neil Kinnock, leader of the Labour party in the 1980s. In 1986 he remembered: 'It had a fitted fridge, a kitchen table that folded into the wall and a bathroom. Family and friends came visiting to view the wonders. It seemed like living in a spaceship.'

The end of the prefab programme has a curiously modern ring to it, involving the value of sterling, overseas debts and the balance of payments. Notwithstanding Labour's concentration on domestic issues after the economically ruinous adventure of the war, it was evident by 1946 that an increased share of the nation's output of goods would have to be diverted into exports so that the international balance of payments could be restored.

Lend-lease, the wartime arrangement under which the United States had supplied Britain with food and raw materials in return for the allocation of greater resources to the war effort, had ended abruptly with the defeat of Japan and had to be replaced by a hastily negotiated £937 million loan, to be repaid over 50 years starting in 1950.

In the summer of 1947, the government allowed the exchange rate against the dollar (pegged at $4.80 since before the war) to float. Within five weeks, the Treasury lost 84 per cent of its dollar reserves. The British gross domestic product, worth 16 times the $2.4 billion reserve held in the spring of 1947, proved inadequate to sustain sterling. Convertibility was abruptly ended, but the crisis showed clearly that the allocation of 60 per cent of the country's resources to house building – which absorbed labour and contributed nothing to exports – was no longer possible.

From 1947 until the 31 per cent devaluation of 1949, everything had to be thrown into an export drive. In the end all the ambitious housing plans of the wartime coalition government, like those of the post-war Labour government, failed, because in the ultimate analysis, housing was just not important enough. ■

Martin Pawley is an architectural writer and critic. (This chapter is based on an article first published in ROOF in 1989).

chapter 11

DIY for the homeless

Ron Bailey

Squatting has had a long history, from 17th century
occupations, through post-war seizing of empty army camps, to
the pitched battles of the 1960s

With the thoughts and words of Gerrard Winstanley for inspiration,
the first squatters occupied and cultivated waste lands in England
in 1649:

> The sin of property we do disdain
> No-one has any right to buy and sell the earth for private gain
> From the men of property the orders came
> They sent the hired men and troopers to wipe out the Diggers'
> claim
> Tear down their cottages, burn down their corn
> They were dispersed but the vision lingers on.

And that vision – of homes (if not land) and freedom for all – does
linger on, over 300 years later. The current squatting 'movement',
although probably having less high ideals than its precursors of 1649,
has achieved one thing that its ancestors did not: survival. It is nearly
30 years since the first tentative squat in an east London luxury block in
December 1968, and the bloody battles of June 1969 when 'hired men'
employed by Redbridge borough council tried to wipe out the
squatters' claim – and failed.

In 1919, soldiers returning from the front found few of the
promised homes fit for heroes and so, to the astonishment and rage of
the government, they seized the empty homes to live in. Nearly 30

Press Association

Happy family: in 1969 the O'Connors became Southwark's 'first squatter family' when they moved into an empty council property after being given notice to quit their privately rented bedsit

years later, a much larger outbreak of squatting occurred, starting in the spring of 1945 in Blantyre, Scotland. In the summer of that year the vigilante movement, consisting largely of homeless ex-servicemen, was installing homeless people in empty properties in many areas, including Southend-on-Sea, Brighton and Hastings.

In May 1946, James Fielding and his family occupied a disused service camp in Scunthorpe, Lincolnshire, and this event sparked off further such occupations. A Squatters Protection Society was born, and soon hundreds of empty camps all over Britain were occupied. There were nearly 45,000 squatters by October 1946.

The movement spread to London and empty flats and hotels were occupied. There were massive street demonstrations. The culmination came that September when an attempt to occupy the Duchess of Bedford Buildings was thwarted by the authorities. Six communist organisers were tried and convicted.

Although this did succeed in stopping the movement in London, four points need to be made as comment. Firstly, it did not stop squatting throughout the country. Secondly, the movement was enormously successful – some 850 empty camps were actually handed over to the squatters by the Ministry of Works. Thirdly, although that particular event was communist-organised, the movement as a whole was certainly not (indeed the party had been cool towards the movement for some time and had even denounced the vigilante groups of a year earlier). And fourthly, it is perhaps significant that it was only the more centrally organised operations that the authorities succeeded against.

In August 1965, Mrs Joan Daniels and her children were occupying homeless family accommodation at King Hill hostel provided by Kent county council. They had been there for three months and were due to be evicted onto the streets in accordance with the rule that prevented them from staying longer. Her children would then be taken into care as they had no home. Joan and her husband Stan, however, were not prepared to allow this. When the welfare officials arrived to carry out their duty they not only found Joan unwilling to go, but also that Stan had moved in (another breach of the rules – no husbands were allowed in this homeless family accommodation) and they had barricaded themselves inside. The officials retreated, promising to return.

Other husbands moved in. More families defied the three-month rule. The Friends of King Hill Hostel was formed. The battle lasted a year before Kent county council was forced to cave in and permit husbands and wives to live together, end the three-month rule and the taking of children into care, and improve conditions at the hostel.

During that year all the might of the state had been used to try to crush the protest; injunctions were taken out against husbands visiting their families – when they defied the ban they were jailed for contempt of court.

But the council lost, despite being united in its attempts to crush the action: Labour councillors joined Conservatives in jailing the homeless. The only exception was the Conservative member for Ramsgate, Kenneth Joseph, who supported the campaign.

The campaign, and publicity given to the jailings, forced the councils to back down; 23 local authorities changed their 'no husbands' rule overnight. More protests followed – in Birmingham, at Abridge hostel in Essex and in Wandsworth. Abridge hostel (a dormitory – two rows of beds, no husbands – 'the worst shit hole this side of hell', as it was described at the time) was closed down after families and supporters moved in with carpenters to partition off the hostel and make separate compartments so that husbands could move in. At first the council tried to crush this, too. But it retreated – scared of another 'King Hill'.

I remember the phone call that Sunday in 1966 with Walter Boyce, the Essex social services director. We were in the hostel and the police had ringed the building. Mr Boyce was adamant. 'Alright, Mr Boyce,' I said, 'we've just finished at King Hill and we're quite ready for the same here...'

'You're the King Hill people?' interrupted Mr Boyce. 'Yes'. A long silence followed. Three days later the council announced the closure of the hostel and the rehousing of the families.

During these struggles, the idea of squatting had been aired by the homeless families themselves, along the lines of: 'If we don't get out of this place we should take over that row of empty houses down the road'.

And we did. First, a token squat on 1 December 1968; a second 24-hour stay on 21 December in an empty vicarage. And finally the big one. The installation of families into empty houses – with the intention of staying. Houses in Ilford in Redbridge were chosen – council-owned; empty for years; due to remain so for another five or more.

We planned everything to the last detail: barricades; furniture; split-second timing; rope ladders; three months' supply of food; camping stoves. We did not know what would happen and we prepared for every eventuality – including the law.

We had researched the law in minute detail and produced a 'legal warning' informing the authorities that they would be breaking the 1381 Statute of Forcible Entry if they evicted us without a court order. I had discovered this law after being charged with it (unsuccessfully) as a result of the earlier occupation of the Greek Embassy. Many months' research went into this legal warning – and it worked. After some initial skirmishes, the police kept out of things.

The council thus had to seek redress in the courts – which they did. But unsuccessfully. We deployed a series of legal manoeuvres and won or evaded all legal attempts to remove us from the houses. For six months during 1969, the struggle was fought with more families joining the squat and the council behaving more outrageously to try to stop it (and, yes, just like Kent and King Hill, the Conservative and Labour groups united in trying to crush the homeless).

For instance, the council sent in workmen to smash up houses by sawing through joists, ripping out ceilings and stripping all the services. These were places in good condition, with up to ten years of life before redevelopment.

At 6am on 21 April 1969, Barrie Quartermaine, a so-called private detective, and his hired thugs appeared on the scene. Their calling card was a crowbar through the front door of the squatters' homes. They then charged up to their bedroom, dragged the squatters out of bed (children and all) and threw their possessions out of the window. When David Jenkins protested they smashed his jaw: he spent six weeks with it wired up. A reign of terror ensued. We were followed on the streets: Olive Mercer, who was pregnant, was chased and smashed in the stomach with an iron bar. She miscarried.

We regrouped, re-occupied and even started to repair houses vandalised by the council. The authorities replied with criminal prosecutions: charging us with entering houses and committing unlawful damage. I submitted to the court that we had entered and committed unlawful repairs. We were acquitted.

So the hired men were called in again – in larger numbers. At 5.30am on 25 June 1969 they arrived. We watched them gather in the street outside. They collected piles of rocks and bricks and bottles from neighbouring houses and at a signal from Quartermaine they attacked. Missiles were hurled at the house and came in through the windows. Luckily we wore helmets and these protected us. Meanwhile, other hired men charged the door with a battering ram and swung grappling irons to erect ladders to try to get in through the windows.

They got in through the door – but we had loosened the floorboards and they fell down into the cellar. So they started a fire to try to burn us out but we doused it with water and tarpaulin. At this point, after 15 minutes of battle, the police stepped in. Inspector David

Millam stopped the fighting as he 'feared a breach of the peace was about to take place'!

We had won. I have preached and practised total non-violence for all my political career *as a principle*, but I cannot see what else we could have done that day. The families were housed and Redbridge entered into negotiations for a short-life housing deal with a local self-help group which we set up.

But it was outside Redbridge that the real effects of this victory were shown. We installed families in empty houses in Lewisham and the council wanted no Redbridge-style repeat. It offered a deal: the squatters could have all the council's empty houses if we agreed to vacate when the time came for redevelopment. The council also agreed to 'point' squatters on their pre-squatting (and therefore worse) accommodation.

The Lewisham Family Squatting Association was born. Interestingly, this first deal with a self-help group was signed by a Conservative council. The Labour minority accused the Tories of 'selling out to the anarchists' and called for a battle. (That argument later went full circle: the organisation became a registered housing co-operative.)

Soon 'legal squatting', or what is now known as 'short-life arrangements', was spreading to properties owned by the Conservative-controlled GLC, Lambeth, Greenwich, Ealing, Camden, Islington and Tower Hamlets. The Communist party, which had supported the Redbridge struggle against the reactionary Tory council, voted with the Labour majority in Tower Hamlets in trying to crush the squatters, as we were 'splitting the working class movement'.

We had to outwit Southwark with legal delaying tactics and publicity. Every statement we made was reasonable. We 'wanted to help the council solve its problems by using houses they had no use for' and we offered to 'do up empty houses for the council's homeless families'. Even when we bit hard it was 'so bloody reasonable', as one councillor complained. Thus we asked the national Labour party to help – by occupying Transport House three days before the local government elections. This 'ultra-reasonable' tactic was, and remains, an effective way in which small groups can defeat powerful authorities.

Gradually Southwark started to behave stupidly – smashing up empty houses, distorting figures and literally lying (we had leaked documents to prove it). We set up a 'respectable' front of 'heavyweights' to offer the council a way off the hook – a deal with Southwark Self Help Housing. What it did not know was that we controlled Southwark Self Help Housing.

The 'legal squatting' deals were working. The Conservative minister of housing, Julian Amery, recommended in 1974 that local authorities made arrangements with short-life groups and 'reliable squatters' organisations'. Thus was the current short-life property movement born.

We probably had four aims when we started back in 1968:
- sparking off a mass 'direct action for homes' movement
- achieving better housing by direct action
- radicalising attitudes to housing
- building a radical alternative housing force.

What developed was a mass movement, although it took longer to develop than we hoped. Even official statistics[1] show that there are between 30,000 and 50,000 squatting in England alone. For many people, squatting is the only answer to homelessness. Whereas 25 years ago no-one would have thought of squatting, now it is one of the answers. This can only be called a political consciousness.

I believe that virtually every improvement in national policy towards the homeless has been achieved by direct action. The authorities have been dragged along squealing; enlightened politicians backed the campaigns readily, and thereby assisted. But the strength and the initiative came because of successful and uncontrolled (and uncontrollable) direct action which has incurred the wrath and opposition of *all* the political parties. ∎

Notes

1. *Squatting: a consultation paper*, Home Office 1991, p3, paras 9-10

Ron Bailey is the parliamentary co-ordinator for Friends of the Earth and for the Association for the Conservation of Energy

chapter 12

Building for the masses

John English

Council housing played a major part in post-war building programmes. How did it move from being the subject of political consensus to a target for spending cuts?

Chapter eight deals with the introduction of state subsidies for council housing in 1919 and the development of the tenure during the inter-war years. By 1939, council housing was established as an important form of provision, accounting for about 10 per cent of the total stock. After 1945, successive governments promoted the building of council housing, though with varying degrees of enthusiasm, and the sector expanded virtually every year until the 1980s. But the housing policies of the Thatcher government meant that a combination of right to buy sales and a low level of new building resulted in its contraction. Council housing declined from a peak of about 30 per cent of the stock in the 1970s, to little more than 20 per cent in the mid-1990s.

Governments of all parties supported the building of council homes, both before and after 1945, for a variety of reasons. Views about the proper role of council housing have varied between the parties and over time. Sometimes it has been as a safety net for the poor and to rehouse people from slum clearance schemes; sometimes as a short-term expedient to get houses built quickly; sometimes as the 'normal' working-class tenure; and, briefly, as a potentially dominant tenure catering for all classes.

Political debates on the appropriate function of council housing can help us to understand how it reached its present state, and to put arguments over the right to buy and 'residualisation' into an historical context.

Built to Last?

Production line: council houses in the shadow of Austin's factory at Longbridge, Birmingham

The housing situation in 1945 resembled that in 1918; although the housing stock had been greatly expanded during the inter-war years, there had been virtually no building for six years, and bomb damage meant severe shortages. There was agreement between the parties that council housing would play a major role in the post-war building programme. The Tories also envisaged a substantial role for private enterprise, to which subsidies would be extended, but Labour wanted local authorities to dominate. Labour won the 1945 election, and proceeded to implement its programme under the leadership of the new minister of health, Aneurin Bevan.

As well as Labour's general pro-public sector ideology, there was a rhetoric of social mixing and rejection of 'one-class' council estates. The statutory restriction of council housing to the 'working classes' was repealed in 1949.

In 1945-51, over four-fifths of the houses completed were for public authorities (mainly local authorities). In 1951, the proportion was running at almost 90 per cent.

At Bevan's insistence, the new council houses were built to high standards, particularly of space. During this period, council housing came as close as it has ever come to being a 'universal' service like the NHS, potentially catering for practically the whole population. But in reality, Bevan's vision for council housing for all never came near to being achieved. Few non-manual worker-headed households have ever been council tenants. In any case, there was already too much owner-occupation – amounting to about a third of the stock – to make it likely that council housing would ever be accepted as a universal service.

The first effect of the Conservative election victory in 1951, when Harold Macmillan was appointed minister of housing, was that the output of council housing increased. It was not that the Tories became enthusiastic about general needs council housing, but the leadership had been bounced into a commitment to building 300,000 houses a year by the party's 1950 conference after criticism of Labour's 'inadequate' record.

The basic Tory position was endorsement of owner-occupation – a 'property-owning democracy' – with council housing in a special needs role. But building for owner-occupation could not be cranked up to a high level, so until 1953/54, local authority output was increased to unprecedented levels. Subsidies were raised, and Macmillan told local authorities to build as many houses as possible.

One way in which Macmillan was able to increase the output of council houses was by reducing space standards (a process started by the Labour government), to economise on bricks and timber. The so-called 'people's house' tends to be criticised as a retrograde step, but these houses have generally been popular and plenty have been bought under the right to buy since 1980.

The 1953 White Paper, *Houses: the next step*, made the government's position clear. 'One object of future housing policy will be to continue to promote, by all possible means, the building of new houses for owner-occupation. While anxious to encourage the spread of house ownership, Her Majesty's Government have been equally conscious of the need for houses to meet the requirements of the greater part – perhaps necessarily the greater part – of the population. They have been careful to secure that the building of more houses to sell shall not prejudice the building of houses to let. This dual policy will be continued.'

In 1954, Duncan Sandys replaced Harold Macmillan at the ministry of housing and once the overall target had been achieved in 1954, local authority output was reduced to below 300,000 for the rest of the decade (on the basis of what the economy could afford).

Private sector completions exceeded those in the public sector in 1958 and, with the exception of a brief period in the late 1960s, have remained in the majority. By the early 1960s, public sector output had settled down to around 40 per cent of the total.

Slum clearance, suspended in 1939, was restarted in 1954 and from then on a substantial proportion of new council houses were used for rehousing. In addition, there was concern about the housing conditions of elderly people, many of whom lived in the private sector, and local authorities were urged to cater for them. The 1956 Housing Subsidies Act withdrew new subsidies for general needs building and limited them to dwellings for rehousing and one-bedroomed units. (The Act also notoriously encouraged high rise building by providing subsidies which increased with storey height).

The last few years of Tory rule up to 1964 were marked by a revival of council building from its low point around 1960. Housing was still a major political issue, and a great deal of argument centred on the rate of slum clearance.

The 1960s were also the era of system-built blocks of flats which were widely seen both as a way of boosting output where skilled labour was in short supply and of rehousing people from slums without undue resort to overspill. No doubt this was all done with the best of (somewhat paternalistic) intentions – it certainly was not a cheap policy – but it has burdened council housing with an appalling legacy of unpopular and difficult-to-let accommodation with which local authorities are currently struggling.

When Labour took office under Harold Wilson, the numbers game was still rampant in housing politics and Labour announced a target of 500,000 houses a year by 1970. (In fact this was never achieved and was abandoned with public expenditure cuts in 1967.) Its 1965 White Paper called for a 'proper balance' between owner-occupation and council housing. The building programme was to be split equally between the two tenures, implying some increase in the relative importance of the public sector but higher output in both. There were to be more generous subsidies for the public sector (introduced in the 1967 Housing Act).

'But once the country has overcome its huge social problem of slumdom and obsolescence,' the White Paper said, 'the programme of subsidised housing should decrease. The expansion of the public sector programme now proposed [is] to meet exceptional needs. The expansion of building for owner-occupation on the other hand is normal; it reflects long-term social advance.' Labour endorsed owner-occupation as the 'normal' tenure and saw the large-scale building of council housing as an essentially short-term expedient to meet 'exceptional' needs.

The 1965 White Paper also reiterated support for the disastrous use of novel construction methods – 'Housebuilding must be increasingly industrialised to get the numbers we need.' 'Parker Morris' standards were to be mandatory for public sector building, providing for better space standards, space heating and so on.

In opposition, the Conservatives had moved towards a more vigorous policy of promoting owner-occupation. Few council houses had been sold before the mid-1960s, but in 1967 and 1968 many urban local authorities were won by the Tories and some (notably Birmingham and the Greater London Council) started enthusiastically to sell properties to tenants.

The Labour government did not oppose sales in principle, but argued that they were inappropriate in areas with high housing need, and so limited sales in many areas. In 1970 the new Conservative government removed these restrictions to encourage council house sales (though, despite backbench prompting, a right to buy was not introduced).

Sales increased, but even in the peak year, 1973, they amounted to only about a third of public sector completions. New building fell back to below the previous low point in 1961, though the public sector continued to expand throughout the period.

The other strand of Conservative policy was the reform of public sector housing subsidies. These were a mess, having been built up over half a century and bearing no relationship to the financial position of particular local authorities. But subsidy reform was used as an opportunity to force up the level of council rents. Better-off tenants would pay more, thus reducing public expenditure, while no doubt encouraging them to consider owner-occupation. At the same time poorer tenants – those who really should be council tenants – would be 'protected' by the new national rent rebate scheme.

Rent increases under the 1972 Housing Finance Act were halted by Labour in 1974. Much the same mix of policies, however – council house sales, higher rents and increased reliance on rebates – was to be used a good deal more effectively by the next Tory government after 1979.

The 1974 Labour government abandoned 'fair' rents in the public sector and existing subsidies were frozen pending the completion of a housing finance (later policy) review, which resulted in the famous Green Paper of 1977. Council housing seemed to be doing well for a brief period: the owner-occupied market moved from boom to slump, there was an increased demand for council housing, and speculative builders were glad to sell completed estates to local authorities.

But the bubble burst by 1976/77: new council building, which had been increased, fell away again under the impact of public expenditure cuts.

The 1977 Green Paper reiterated successive governments' support for owner-occupation. A right to buy (promised by the Conservative opposition) was rejected and rent increases were to be in line with average earnings, but the comments on tenure were not drastically different from the position of the Tory government after 1979. 'An increasing number of people want to own their own home,' the paper said. 'The Government welcome this trend. For most people owning one's home is a basic and natural desire, which for more and more people is becoming attainable.' The Green Paper recognised that 'one of the consequences of the continuing growth and wider access to home ownership could be gradually to narrow the social make-up of the public rented sector.'

In fact, the residualisation of council housing was already well under way. The Labour cabinet apparently considered adopting the right to buy and so stealing a popular Tory policy.

The right to buy was initially controversial. Some councils tried to delay its implementation, and for a time Labour promised to repeal it. But within a few years it was accepted by all parties and it has become a permanent feature of British housing. Over one and a half million public sector (mainly council) houses have been sold, and the public sector fell from just under a third of the housing stock in 1979 to little more than a fifth in 1991.

The 1980 Housing Act was largely a rerun of an abortive bill introduced by Labour shortly before they lost office, with the addition of the right to buy. Both included new rights for public sector tenants such as security of tenure. Exchequer subsidy was to be reduced on the basis of government assumptions about annual rent increases – local authorities had little alternative but to raise rents.

By the mid-1980s, the government had succeeded in its immediate objectives. But a great many council houses remained which were not going to be purchased by individual tenants. The future of rented housing was reviewed, and the 1987 White Paper, *Housing: the government's proposals*, proposed that housing subsidies were to be 'reformed' again and housing revenue accounts 'ring-fenced'.

The Conservative government's long-term objective was that local authorities should eventually cease to be landlords, transferring their stock to housing associations or local housing companies (not-for-profit social landlords, which unlike housing associations, include local authority nominees on their boards). Local authority responsibility in housing would be confined to a 'strategic' or 'enabling' role. Transfers began on a modest scale during the 1990s, but shortly before they lost office in 1997 the Conservatives announced that councils would be required to bring forward plans to transfer the whole of their housing stocks. These proposals are not being pursued by the Labour government, though stock transfers on a voluntary basis will continue.

As owner-occupation has grown, it has attracted large numbers of more or less affluent working-class households which were once the backbone of council housing: partly through the right to buy but in the long-term more importantly through the tenure choices of new households. The tenure has increasingly become dominated by households outside the labour market – the elderly, long-term sick, unemployed and single parents, most of which are dependent on social security benefits. There are two reasons for this trend: the massive decline in the private rented sector and the growth in the size of these groups. These trends have been summed up as the 'residualisation' of council housing. One cannot say that residualisation began at a specific time, and it was certainly under way in the 1970s before the right to buy which simply accelerated the process.

It is sometimes said that council housing – and to a large extent housing association housing is not much different – is becoming, to use an American term, 'welfare housing'. Social rented housing in Britain is still very different from the tiny and highly stigmatised public sector in the United States, although similarities are clear in some of the most deprived and difficult-to-let estates. A different system of housing subsidies, which made the choice between renting and buying financially more equal for non-poor households, might have allowed council housing to be an attractive alternative to owner-occupation for those able to exercise choice. But that is water under the bridge: council housing has a very different role in the housing system in the 1990s than in the 1950s and 1960s. Mass owner-occupation is far too entrenched in Britain for a return to council housing as anything but part of the social housing safety net to be conceivable.

Council housing has lost the positive image it once possessed and most of its political constituency; Labour's enthusiasm for it is more lukewarm than ever, a far cry from the days of Aneurin Bevan. Getting a council house may be a lifeline for the homeless, single parents and others without choice, but most people do have choice and few of them seriously consider social renting. Owner-occupation went through a rocky patch in the first half of the 1990s, with high interest rates, falling house prices and mortgage default, but all the signs are that things are getting back to normal and home ownership is as popular as ever. The Labour government, despite its early policy of severe constraints on public expenditure, introduced legislation to 'release' capital receipts from council house sales; this is likely to be modestly beneficial, though the additional capital expenditure will often be used for repair and rehabilitation of the existing stock rather than new build.

Housing tenure has been changing at least since the 1920s, and one can only speculate about the future. But it does seem quite likely that we may now be entering a period of comparative stability. Owner-occupation in England and Wales has been fairly stable for a number of years, and, particularly with a Labour government which has less of a fetish for home ownership than its predecessor, the tenure may stick at around 70 per cent of the stock (though there is probably still potential for further growth from a lower base in Scotland). A small private rented sector, operating essentially in niche markets, is unlikely to fall below its current ten per cent or so share. That would leave social housing with some 20 per cent of the stock (more north of the border). Even the last Conservative government did not seem seriously to believe that this represented much more than an irreducible minimum, though they would have liked to get it out of the hands of local authorities.

At the moment social housing is predominantly council housing, and following the change of government may well remain so. But transfer of council estates to housing associations and, particularly in large towns and cities, local housing companies, will continue; apart from anything else these landlords have access to private borrowing which is a significant advantage when public sector capital expenditure is being severely squeezed.

A substantial public sector is likely to remain for a long time. The tasks of housing departments were once mainly routine, such as the collection of rents and organisation of repairs. Now there is a major element of individual care and supervision which requires different skills from staff. Many management tasks, for the frail elderly, the mentally ill, or disabled people, are really an aspect of care in the community. Other tasks relate to coping with the limited personal and social competence of many younger tenants.

The role of council housing has constantly evolved over the years. A large public sector may be seen as an essentially transitional phase in housing provision which was required when the private rented sector was in decline but the extension of owner-occupation to the bulk of the population did not seem feasible. Mistakes have been made, but overall, council housing has made a major contribution to improving housing conditions in Britain. One thing that is certain is that the role of council housing will continue to evolve. ■

John English is lecturer in social policy at the Department of Applied Social Studies, University of Paisley

chapter 13

No welcome home

Susan Smith and Sara Hill

Far from being welcomed with open arms, post-war migrants from the West Indies and Asia faced discrimination and racism in every housing sector

In 1948, Britain passed a Nationality Act. It was the price paid for creating Commonwealth from Empire, and it entitled the people of the ex-colonies to British citizenship. The right to live and work in Britain, protected by the law and insured by the welfare state, was part of this package. So, of course, was an obligation to pay tax and to live within the law.

But the story since 1948 has been one of political compromise, with the state extracting obligations while curtailing entitlements. The social history of housing – the negotiable right to shelter – provides a sobering illustration. After the second world war, Britain, like so many other European countries, had an urgent need for cheap labour. Traditionally, we are told that the government recruited West Indian (and later south Asian) migrants, and welcomed them with open arms.

Cabinet papers tell a rather different tale. The government did everything it could to recruit migrant workers from anywhere *but* the New Commonwealth. It preferred European workers: displaced people from Germany, Austria and Italy, East European refugees, and anyone else who the Royal Commission on Population (reporting in 1949) could be sure 'were of good human stock and not prevented by their religion or race from intermarrying with the host population and becoming merged with it.'

The preference was for migrants who were not citizens, and had no right of abode or entitlement to welfare. The government wanted workers who would not compound the 'threat' of ghettos becoming established in the port areas, and who would be more 'fitted' than 'colonial peoples' to the kinds of jobs available.

In the end, the demands of the economy won, and colonial immigration was encouraged. But scarcely had the invitation been issued than the cabinet turned its attention to future immigration controls. Throughout the 1950s, administrative arrangements discriminated against black immigrants. Strict proof of British nationality was demanded, shipping lists were tampered with to put migrant workers at the back of the queue, passports were delayed, and travel certificates were often faulty.

With this ambivalence towards black citizens, it is easier to understand (though not to justify) why no attempt was made in those early years to co-ordinate immigration with housing policy. Migration to Britain was initially seen as numerically limited, short-lived and, crucially, temporary. As MP Harold Davies put it, when discussing the role of 'colonial' workers: 'Having helped our productivity and output, that manpower or womanpower could go back to the Colonies and be a nucleus of productivity there.' (*Hansard* 1946-47, vol.441, col.1415).

It was never expected that the migrants would stay, and governments did not encourage them to do so by providing homes. Employers received no incentive to find homes for their workers (in contrast to the pattern in several other European countries).

Politicians would not formally entertain the possibility that the white British public, or the institutions in which they worked, might discriminate against black households. Britain was, after all, a world leader in tolerance and understanding: racism was a problem for foreign, not domestic policy. Thus, despite the efforts of Fenner Brockway and a few Labour party colleagues (who annually introduced a Bill to outlaw discrimination from 1956), the 1950s and much of the 1960s passed with no serious concern for the difficulties black (Afro-Caribbean and Asian) people had in finding accommodation. There was no legal protection for those denied a home because of the colour of their skin. Yet, throughout this period, homes *were* denied on racial grounds in every sector of the housing system.

The private rented sector was often the migrants' first port of call. By the late 1940s, it was already a residual sector for the white

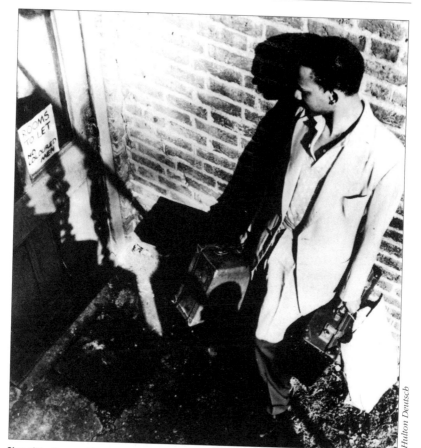

Hulton Deutsch

Sign of the times: a black man looking for accommodation in 1958. Signs like 'no coloureds' were legal until 1968

population. Properties were often old, in poor repair, reserved for multiple occupation and located in the inner city.

Private renting was often the only option for Afro-Caribbean and, later, Asian migrants. But this was by no means an open sector. The exclusionary banner: 'No blacks, no Irish, no dogs' was quite legal until 1968, and even in that year, the clause 'no coloureds' was included in more than a quarter of adverts for rented accommodation placed in a local newspaper circulating in London's East End (*The Guardian*, 2 August, 1968). Stories like that of Tony Overman, who rented a double room in a boarding house but was asked to leave because his wife was black (*Daily Herald*, 1 January, 1954), abound in the press cuttings of the 1950s.

Even in 1964, over half the rented properties in Oxford were unavailable to African or Asian students (*The Guardian*, 26 November, 1964) and in 1965, the Milner Holland report indicated that only a third of private landlords in London would let their dwellings to 'coloured' tenants.

It has been suggested that, as a consequence of discrimination, a split market occurred in private renting. Black people were effectively restricted to properties owned by black landlords, and this pushed up rents and encouraged overcrowding. For this, and other reasons, black tenants in the private sector have always had accommodation of lower than average quality, in which they must live at higher than average densities, for greater than average rents.

As the 1950s unfolded, public housing became a cornerstone of the welfare state and it promised a solution to the post-war housing shortage. Local authorities were required to allocate homes according to need, rather than ability to pay. By virtue of their low incomes and housing needs (especially when joined by their families), New Commonwealth migrants should have been eligible for council homes. However, in the procedures adopted to determine housing need, it was soon apparent that white people's needs were to be ranked above those of their black counterparts.

Even by the mid-1960s, only six per cent of the overseas-born black population had secured access to council housing, compared with 28 per cent of Irish migrants and about one third of the rest of the population. Something was preventing black people from getting council housing – the reluctance of local politicians and white communities to allow black citizens equal welfare benefits.

The early 1960s saw a rash of colour bar petitions submitted to councillors by white council tenants. The example of the Loughborough Road Estate in Brixton is reported in the *Daily Mail* (28 September, 1964). Five hundred tenants complained about the allocation of a two-bedroomed maisonette to a black family. Their spokesperson is quoted as saying: 'There are many British families who need a home without it being given to immigrants. We have a nice housing estate here and that's how we want it to stay.' The same sentiments were expressed by the occupants of Bank Street Flats, Wolverhampton, who threatened to leave *en masse* when they discovered a flat was to be let to a black family (*Daily Express*, 6 June, 1966).

This notion that the citizenship rights of 'coloured' immigrants did not extend to living in council housing was more often reinforced than resisted by the councils themselves. (Though it is important to recognise that in recent years, many local authorities have spearheaded the anti-racist housing movement.) In 1965, the Smethwick housing management committee is reported to have recommended that a new 15-storey block of flats should not be made available to black families because 'when people find coloured people moving in they become apprehensive' (Committee chairman, cited in *The Times*, 5 May, 1966). In 1966, the Birmingham borough Labour conference openly rejected a proposal to allocate council houses on new estates to black applicants.

Apart from this overt policy of exclusion, housing departments often imposed access rules which effectively prevented black families from queuing for a council home on equal terms with white applicants. The most notorious of these were residence requirements, which meant that people had to live in the area for a number of years before being allowed onto council waiting lists. This obviously excluded recent immigrants, and today, such requirements are recognised in law as indirect discrimination.

Residence requirements were justified in a variety of ways. As the chair of Wolverhampton's housing committee put it in 1967: 'It seems reasonable to us that if someone comes to this country, they should wait two years. They may not like it here and may go back.' (*The Times*, 9 September, 1967). In Birmingham, a five-year residence requirement was retained until 1977, and it has been suggested by some researchers that demand from local whites was systematically exaggerated to keep this rule in place, to limit the number of black applicants admitted to the housing lists.

By the mid-1960s, white households were 26 times more likely than their black counterparts to have secured a council home. This was hardly a reflection of differences in housing need, but local politicians preferred a happy electorate to an open housing system. Patricia

Hornsby-Smith MP observed that: 'If the housing committees allocated their property exclusively on the basis of social need, no white family would get anywhere near an allocation for the next ten or 15 years.' (*Hansard* 1971, vol.813, col.118).

Such exclusion needed a response. A vigorous black housing association movement was established, and it flourished towards the end of the 1950s. This succeeded for some years in filling at least part of the housing gap for black people. Some of these associations later catered to a wider public, but many closed or were taken over by large 'white' associations following the 1974 Housing Act. It was only more recently that the Housing Corporation recognised the importance of black-led initiatives and started working with black people to rekindle the black housing association movement.

Excluded from the public sector, discriminated against in the private rented sector, many Asian and (to a lesser extent) Afro-Caribbean households turned to home-ownership. Here they faced discrimination in applying for mortgages, and their choice of homes was further limited by the activities of estate agents, as well as by resistance from existing white owners.

In the absence of legislation against discrimination, the Bradford Equitable building society was able, in 1957, to explain in writing to a 37-year-old Jamaican civil servant and LSE graduate that: 'It is the policy of the society's directors not to approve advances to coloured people' (*Sunday Pictorial*, 21 July, 1957). Others may not have been so open, but research shows conventional mortgage finance was (and for many years remained) denied to black people. In the 1960s, it was possible for estate agents to respond to the demands of groups like the Southall residents' association, which, in 1963, claimed that 'the problems these immigrants are introducing are numerous and too apparent' and wrote to estate agents asking them to 'restrain your activities with regard to coloured people' (*The Times,* 9 November, 1963).

It was also possible, and legal, for a Wolverhampton property developer to ban the sale of 300 new houses to 'coloured' families (*The Guardian*, 12 August, 1965). And it was possible for the Rowley Regis residents' association in Staffordshire to ask to buy the home of a local Jamaican family on the grounds that 'we do not want coloured people on our estate. We do not want the value of our property to diminish.'

(Chairman of Rowley Regis residents' association, cited in the *Daily Mail*, 31 May, 1965).

As a consequence of low incomes and discrimination, black people found cheap homes in the inner and middle rings of the major cities, usually in areas scheduled for clearance or blighted by short leases. Their dependence on 'unconventional' loans (often over short periods with high repayments and high interest rates) excluded them from tax concessions. Their homes were often costly to maintain and repair, yet research shows that they made relatively limited capital gains through several periods of house price inflation.

Politicians knew the difficulties facing black Britons during the 1950s and early 1960s. The Attlee Cabinet considered the problems of discrimination in employment and housing. In 1955, a Conservative Cabinet also acknowledged that: 'The most serious problem arising at present from coloured immigration is undoubtedly in the field of housing.' But the response was not to legislate against discrimination, or to intervene in other ways, but to introduce immigration controls which infringed the entitlements of black Britons even more.

Politicians had always feared the development of 'racial' segregation. It suggested colour bars and civil unrest. But by the late 1950s, the segregation of black people, socially and geographically, into some of Britain's worst housing, had already happened. In parliament though, segregation, poor housing, unemployment, overcrowding and deprivation were depicted simply as the consequence of having too many 'coloured colonials' packed into too little space. This, it was argued, was an environmental hazard, a drain on resources, and a threat to the urban landscape. As a problem of numbers and location, the solution seemed obvious.

This solution, claimed the Conservatives after their annual conference in 1961, was to restrict immigration. The benefits would include the integration and dispersal of those already settled, and it would help solve the housing problem as well. It was also a vote winner, appealing to the 'common sense' of a public still gripped by the moral panic whipped up from the 1958 Notting Hill riots. And controls would help Britain's entry to the EEC, since they would protect European housing and labour markets from any future influx of Commonwealth migrants.

Built to Last?

The 1962 Commonwealth Immigration Act was not passed because it made economic sense, and the Labour party opposed the Act on grounds of economic irrationality. The Act was passed because it proposed to solve a crisis of 'race relations' which was emerging in the inner cities. As Rab Butler, then Conservative home secretary, put it: 'The greater the numbers coming into the country, the larger will these communities become and the more difficult it will be to integrate them into our national life. There is a real risk that the drive for improved conditions will be defeated by the sheer weight of numbers' (*Hansard* 1961, vol.649, cols.694-5). So the right of abode, guaranteed in 1948, was restricted in 1962. Britain failed (on that occasion) to enter the EEC, but the policies of 'race' generally had moved to centre stage.

Matters came to a head in the October 1964 general election. Harold Wilson spoke out on *Panorama* against the slogan allegedly adopted by Conservative candidate, Peter Griffiths. Griffiths was said to be fighting for Smethwick on the platform: 'If you want a nigger [for your] neighbour, vote Labour,' and in a surprise victory, he snatched the seat from Labour's Gordon Walker. The racist vote had become an electoral advantage. Despite Wilson later labelling Griffiths a 'parliamentary leper' when he took his seat, there was no incentive for politicians to press for a more open system.

In 1968, Enoch Powell, publicly lamented 'the transformation of whole areas into alien territory' (Birmingham speech, 20 April, 1968). In that same year, the Labour party relinquished its unpopular opposition to immigration control, and moved swiftly to limit the entry of Asians fleeing persecution in Kenya. An uneasy consensus had been achieved.

Labour justified its U-turn by introducing two Race Relations Acts, in 1965 and 1968. These were to act with immigration restrictions to promote integration (which was still thought to hinge on dispersal). But these Acts were too little, and too late. The marginal housing position of black people had already been established, and the 1965 Act neglected to address discrimination in housing and employment in any case! The second Act remedied this, but indirect discrimination was not outlawed until 1976. No attempt was made to co-ordinate this legislation with housing and urban policy, and for at least ten years, achievements were limited.

The seeds of entrenched racial inequalities in housing –

inequalities which exist even today (sometimes in a different form, and sometimes via different mechanisms) – were sown over 40 years ago. They were sown through politicians' dogged insistence that racism was alien to the British character, by their obsession with the idea that anti-discrimination laws were tantamount to a colour bar, and by an ill-founded (but politically convenient) assumption that early patterns of segregation – and the housing problems embedded in them – could best be solved by immigration controls. The rights given to black Britons in 1948 were never fully exercised and have been compromised by a tendency to manage the housing and legal systems with an eye to political expediency rather than social justice. ■

Susan Smith is a professor of geography at the University of Edinburgh. Sara Hill is a research associate at the Public Health Research and Resource Centre, University of Salford

chapter 14

Burying Rachman

Peter Kemp

The 1957 Rent Act sparked a furious political row over the role
of the private rented sector. This intensified with media interest
in the activities of notorious landlord Peter Rachman

Until very recently, debates about the future of private renting in
Britain have been dogged by stereotypical images of private
landlords and highly polarised political debates. The controversy
surrounding the sector has raged most fiercely during parliamentary
debates on bills to strengthen rent regulation or to introduce decontrol.
Never were the debates so furious as when the bill that became the
1957 Rent Act made its way through parliament.

At that time, the sector was declining rapidly. Both the existing
stock of privately rented dwellings and newly constructed ones were
subject to a stringent form of rent control. The rents of most privately
rented dwellings had not been increased since the war – yet incomes,
repair costs and house prices had all increased substantially in real
terms. As a result, the yield on rental properties had declined
considerably. In many cases, it was just not an economic proposition
for landlords to undertake significant repair and improvement works.

Despite the rapid decline of the sector, by 1957 about a third of
all households were renting their homes from private landlords. They
therefore represented a sizeable constituency of voters which
politicians could ignore at their peril. While the post-war housing
shortage had begun to abate, there remained a substantial excess of
households over dwellings. It was in the private rented sector that the
pressures of housing shortage were most acutely felt. At the same time,
the condition of much of the pre-1919 stock of dwellings, most of

Built to Last?

Popperfoto

Peter Rachman: the slum landlord who made a fortune from his rented properties in London

which were rented privately, was very poor. The post-war slum clearance campaign had only recently got underway and improvement grants had not yet made much of an impression on substandard dwellings outside slum clearance areas.

A last-ditch attempt to revive private investment in rented housing, the 1957 Rent Act was one of the most controversial measures passed by the Macmillan government. Indeed, the parliamentary debates during the passage of the Act were said to have a curious air of unreality about them.[1] Little was then known about private landlords, and both parties relied on caricatures and oversimplified analyses.

For the Tories, rent control was the cause of the decline of private renting. Remove rent controls, they argued, and rents would increase (but not too much, since the post-war housing shortage had eased by then). Higher rents would mean larger profits for landlords and, therefore, an increase in the supply of private lettings. It was all as simple as an elementary lesson in basic economics. Left to itself, the private market would produce the goods – the supply of, and demand for, rented houses would reach an equilibrium. Both landlords and tenants would benefit – one from higher profits, the other from an increased supply of houses to rent.

Labour, in contrast, portrayed the 1957 Rent Act as a 'vicious' piece of class legislation that would profit landlords, but cause serious hardships for tenants, without increasing the supply of rented homes. Rent controls were a necessary safeguard against the all-too-common tendency of private landlords to charge exorbitant rents and exploit their tenants, especially in the face of the housing shortage which still existed in areas like inner London. For many Labour MPs, the decline of private renting was inevitable, even desirable. The answer was not decontrol, but municipalisation of the remaining stock and an expansion of council housebuilding, the subsidies for which had been cut back by the Conservatives in 1956.

The 1957 Rent Act had three main measures. First, all of the more expensive housing was decontrolled at once. This applied to all dwellings with a rateable value of over £40 in London and £30 elsewhere. Second, less expensive houses became decontrolled when the sitting tenant left, a procedure known in the trade as 'creeping decontrol'. And third, the maximum rent that a landlord could charge on property that remained in control was raised to more or less twice the rateable value.

The Act's impact was, generally speaking, much less dramatic than either of the alternative scenarios predicted. A Rowntree housing study, led by the London School of Economics' David Donnison, found that many landlords did put up their rents (some by a considerable amount), but others did not. Decontrol did not produce an increase in investment in rented housing. Rather, disinvestment continued and, indeed, it seems the rate of decline increased, rather than decreased (see Table 1). The average decline in the 62 months up to June 1956 was 236,000 dwellings a year. Between 1956 and 1961, the privately rented sector declined from more than a third to only a quarter of the total stock.

Decontrol provided many landlords with the opportunity to get out of the sector by selling to owner-occupiers, including their own sitting tenants. At the same time, most of the dwellings demolished in slum clearance schemes were owned by private landlords.

It was not until the early 1960s that many of the darker consequences of decontrol became apparent, partly because some of its provisions were postponed until 1961. By then, the housing shortage in places like inner London had become quite severe, especially at the bottom end of the market. With controlled rents well below market levels, creeping decontrol meant that landlords had an incentive to remove their sitting tenants by whatever means they could in order to charge a higher rent. In the late 1950s and early 1960s, stories began to appear in the local press about intimidation of tenants, evictions and homelessness.

What transformed the situation, however, was the storm of publicity surrounding the west London landlord Peter Rachman. His nefarious activities came to light in the wake of the Profumo 'sex and security' scandal in 1963. It turned out that one of the call girls involved in the scandal had earlier been Rachman's mistress. The addition of slum landlordism to the already potent media cocktail of sex and national security allowed the press to inject new life into the Profumo affair. The fact the Rachman was dead by then conveniently removed fears of libel writs that might otherwise have restrained the media. For two weeks, the public was fed a daily dose of stories about the violence and intimidation Rachman was said to have used against tenants.

Sorting out the myths from the facts about Rachman may not be easy, but some things are known. Born in Poland in 1919, he came to England in 1946. According to the Milner Holland report, he first became a landlord in 1954, having acquired four houses in Shepherds Bush. Gradually, he built up a portfolio of rented houses (the precise number is not known), mostly in the Notting Hill area in west London. Many of these properties were in poor condition but, because of the shortage of rented housing, he was able to let them at very high rents once he had got rid of the sitting tenants. Many of his tenants were alleged to be prostitutes.

By the late 1950s, Rachman was being investigated by the police for dealing in prostitution, by the Inland Revenue for tax evasion, and by public health officials about the state of his properties. The ownership of his dwellings was held by over 20 companies between which he continually transferred them. Evading the authorities became increasingly difficult, and by 1961 Rachman had disposed of almost all of his rented houses. He died in 1962, leaving £72,830 before tax.

Labour made considerable political capital out of the episode, and the ailing Macmillan government was forced to set up the Milner

Table 1: Number of private rented homes 1951-1961		
Date	Homes	% total stock
April 1951	6.2 m	45%
June 1956	5.4m	36%
December 1961	4.1m	25%

Source: Report of the Committee on the Rent Acts, 1971 (all figures estimates)

Holland committee to investigate London's housing problems. Harold Wilson, the new, dynamic, young leader of the Labour opposition, claimed that the Rachman saga summed up all that was wrong with the ageing Conservative government. Echoing a view perhaps held by many people in the Labour party at the time, he even argued that 'rented housing was not a proper field for private profit'.

The Milner Holland committee's report, published in 1965, concluded that there was an acute shortage of rented housing in London. The surveys commissioned by the committee found that most tenants were satisfied with the way their landlords treated them, but also that landlord abuse was too common to be dismissed as an isolated problem. The 1964 Labour government attributed its electoral success in part to housing, and passed a new Rent Act in 1965. This Act introduced regulated tenancies and 'fair rents' assessed by independent rent officers in the privately rented housing market. The system remained intact for a quarter of a century until the Conservatives' 1988 Housing Act deregulated new lettings.

The ghost of Rachman has long haunted debates on the future of private renting. He came to symbolise the unacceptable face of private landlordism in Britain and gave to the English language a new word – Rachmanism – to describe the conduct of landlords who charge exorbitant rents for slum housing. So deeply engrained has been the unsavoury image attached to landlordism that respectable private institutions have, ever since, been wary of investing in houses to let. This has arguably been just as important a factor in the sector's stagnation as any fear that a new government might re-regulate lettings.

All this has begun to change. During the 1980s and early 1990s, successive Conservative ministers set about trying to rehabilitate the private landlord's image to inject new life into the sector. In both of these objectives, they had some success. After decades of almost continuous decline, since the early 1980s there has been a mini-revival in the size of the sector. This revival has been facilitated by rent deregulation and changes to security of tenure, but also the early 1990s slump in the owner-occupied housing market.

Something approaching a consensus has begun to develop about the future of private renting. It is becoming increasingly accepted that the private landlord has a number of important roles to play in housing provision, particularly in relation to young, new and mobile households. The new Labour government has promised not to re-introduce rent controls or to reverse the other changes to landlord and tenant law introduced by the previous administration. This has reduced the political risk of investment in the sector and may help to encourage new landlords to enter the market. It seems that the legacy of Peter Rachman – and ideologically-driven debate – has been cast off. Perhaps a more balanced approach has begun to inform policy towards the privately rented sector at last.■

Notes

1. J B Cullingworth, *Essays on housing policy*, Allen & Unwin, 1979

Peter Kemp is director of the ESRC Centre for Housing Research and Urban Studies at the University of Glasgow

chapter 15

The road from Clay Cross

Peter Malpass

The refusal of Clay Cross councillors to implement the 1972 Housing Finance Act was a landmark in the battle to defend the principle of local autonomy in setting council rents

On 1 April 1974, Clay Cross urban district council ceased to exist. In the nationwide reorganisation of local government, this small mining town became a mere part of the new district of North East Derbyshire. But the events of the previous two years meant that the name of Clay Cross would survive as a symbol of local resistance to the power of central government.

The story of the Clay Cross councillors' refusal to implement the fair rent provision of the Conservative government's 1972 Housing Finance Act is a saga of defiant determination to defend the living standards of council tenants and the rights of duly elected representatives to decide policy for their locality. For a year after all other authorities had bowed to the apparently inevitable rent increases, the Labour-controlled Clay Cross council stood alone and continued its battle, in spite of the measures taken against it by the government and the lack of support from the national leadership of the Labour party.

The Housing Finance Act, and Clay Cross's part in its undoing, raised fundamental questions about the nature of local authority housing. More widely, the episode raised questions about circumstances in which citizens in a democracy can justifiably defy laws passed by parliament.

In housing terms, the issues were about the level of council rents, the principle of means-testing as the primary method of determining entitlement to subsidy, and the freedom of local councils

Built to Last?

The Clay Cross rebel eleven: Labour held all 11 seats on the council, due in part to its rents policy

to determine their own housing policy. Given that the government was determined to raise rents and to remove local autonomy in rent setting, both of which were widely opposed in the country at large, the issue then was: how could opposition be mobilised and made effective, and how far could local authorities reasonably pursue their opposition to the law?

These issues and the lessons of the early 1970s are of continuing relevance. In the early 1990s, there was another bout of centrally imposed rent increases, followed by policies designed to hold down the rise of rents, so that although councils formally retain the right to set rents, they can effectively do so only within limits set by the government.

Although the stand taken by Clay Cross in 1972-74 was important then, and remains relevant now, it is necessary to learn from the Housing Finance Act episode as a whole.

The story began with the election of a Conservative government in June 1970, and the appointment of Peter Walker as the first secretary of state at the newly formed Department of the Environment. Walker was an established advocate of the extension of 'fair rents' into the public sector. In July 1971 he published a white paper, *Fair deal for housing*, in which it was argued that housing problems such as slums, overcrowding, dilapidation and individual hardship, could be cured only by a radical reform of housing finance.

The main objective was to establish a uniform system of fair rents for all public and private sector tenants. On the one hand, the government wanted to hasten the replacement of very low controlled rents in the private sector by much higher fair rents, with their built-in tendency to rise in line with inflation. On the other hand, it wanted to raise council rents from levels which were perceived by ministers to be kept unacceptably low by the politically motivated policies of Labour-controlled local councils and a perverse subsidy system.

In this context, the government view was that fairness required all rents to be set in the same way, using the criteria for fair rents introduced for the private sector by the Labour government in 1965. It therefore proposed an entirely new system of subsidies for council housing – central government assistance would be related to the deficit on the housing revenue account, after income from fair rents had been set against expenditure on loan charges, repairs and maintenance.

It was quite clear that the transition to fair rents would lead to some very considerable rent increases around the country, and thus to a substantial saving in central government subsidy. However, the savings were to be offset to some extent by the introduction of a mandatory scheme of rent rebates for low-income council tenants (and a similar scheme, called 'rent allowances', for private tenants). This was presented by ministers as a shift from indiscriminate subsidy of houses to a more targeted and fairer system of subsidising people.

In terms of pricing policy, fair rents represented an attempt to break away from historic costs as the basis for rent setting, and to substitute a system based on current market value. The opposition, however, described the proposals as a vicious attack on working-class living standards and a crude attempt to cut public expenditure behind a smokescreen of rhetoric about fairness.

From the point of view of local councillors, the scale of implied rent increases was matched in importance by the way in which the proposed system removed all local authority discretion to set rents in line with locally determined housing policy. For 50 years, local authorities had considerable autonomy to set council house rents (although regional variations were more closely related to the scale and timing of new building rather than rent policies *per se*). Councils had also enjoyed complete freedom to decide whether to have a rent rebate scheme, and the form and generosity of any scheme.

Built to Last?

Under the terms of the new system set out in the white paper, authorities would have a duty to set provisional fair rents for all their dwellings, but the final decision would lie with a special independent committee for each area. The members of these committees would be drawn from the same panel of people who adjudicated on private sector fair rents.

Thus the long established tradition of local autonomy in rent fixing was undermined in two ways. First, by the requirement to adopt the contentious market-based, fair rent criteria, which many local councillors and supporters of council housing saw as completely inappropriate in the public sector. Second, by denying local authorities the right to be the final arbiters of fair rents in their area. In future, council rents would effectively be set by non-elected, non-accountable committees entirely separate from local authorities themselves.

The government's initial assumption was that fair rents would be substantially above existing rent levels. It therefore required authorities to make a series of annual increases, equivalent to 50p per week, until fair rents were reached. Nowadays, a 50p rent increase may seem modest, but in 1972 it represented an increase of around 25 per cent for most tenants. It should also be remembered that the idea of a rent increase *every* year was not then as well established nor as widely accepted as it has since become.

It was not surprising, therefore, that councillors and tenants in Clay Cross and a great many other places were outraged by the prospect of substantial, compulsory, rent increases every year for the foreseeable future. The Labour party was strongly opposed to the principle of fair rents in the public sector, and from the second reading of the Housing Finance Bill in November 1971, Labour was committed to repealing the fair rents provisions affecting local authorities. In parliament, the opposition fought the Bill by tabling no fewer than 581 amendments in the 57 sittings of the standing committee. But delaying tactics had only nuisance value and the government of course secured its legislation.

The real opposition took place outside parliament at the local level. In a move which paralleled the stance of the Labour leadership on the poll tax, the Labour party leaders in 1972 refused to support local authorities which defied the law and refused to implement the rent increases. Without a clear lead from the parliamentary party, local authority opposition failed to coalesce into an effective force. Nevertheless, the Housing Finance Act brought the issue of council rents to a level of political prominence never previously achieved and the scale of local opposition was impressive. A contemporary observer described it like this:

'Literally thousands of marches, demonstrations, pickets and meetings were held in which hundreds of thousands of people took part. Millions of leaflets were distributed all over the country and large numbers of organisations were set up to co-ordinate the opposition. Hundreds of Labour councillors, by initially refusing to implement the Act, laid themselves open to surcharges and disqualifications from public office. Even when all but a very few Labour councillors capitulated to one or other of the battery of central government threats, up to one hundred thousand local authority tenants continued to struggle against the Act by refusing at one time or another to pay the increase imposed under it.'[1]

At first, more than 100 authorities declared their intention to ignore the Act. But one by one they changed their position, until in October 1972, when the first increases were due, fewer than 50 remained. None of the big urban authorities, apart from the London borough of Camden, carried its opposition into 1973. Eventually there were only two authorities where the councillors adamantly refused to implement the Act.

One was the small South Wales authority of Bedwas and Machen, where the secretary of state for Wales used his power to install a commissioner to take over the housing duties of the local authority. Within three months of the Act taking effect, the commissioner was in position and continued to collect higher rents until 1974.

The other rebel authority was Clay Cross, which differed from most councils in that the Labour party held all 11 seats on the council.[2] This position of strength was largely based on the local party's housing policy, which included low rents. Well before the Act took effect in October 1972, Clay Cross council had made clear its refusal to implement the rent increases. If the government wanted higher rents, then the councillors took the view that the government would have to be seen to be carrying out its own policy, and this meant installing a housing commissioner. However, the government's first action was to declare Clay Cross in default of its duties, and to give a deadline for compliance. This was followed in November 1972 by an audit of the council's accounts, resulting in councillors being personally surcharged and automatically debarred from their positions. The district auditor's decision was appealed against in the High Court in London, where the appeal was lost, with costs awarded against the Clay Cross councillors. It was not until October 1973, a year after the Act came into force, that a commissioner was finally appointed to take over housing administration in the town.

The opposition did not end, however, and the authority refused to co-operate with the commissioner, forcing him to establish his office in nearby Chesterfield. It was the proud boast of the council that in six months, the commissioner failed to collect a single pound of extra rent from tenants in Clay Cross.

The 11 rebel councillors lost their last court battle in January 1974 and finally accepted disqualification from office. Elections were held, and ten of the 11 seats were won by supporters of the Labour rebels, but within two weeks the council was abolished by reorganisation.

It is tempting to see the Clay Cross story as an indication that strength and determination can win through, even against the might and power of central government. It is also worth noting that the government was slow to act against Clay Cross, and never actually used all the powers at its disposal.

On the other hand, the fame of Clay Cross derives from the fact that it was the only authority in England to take a defiant position, and it is important to consider why other authorities failed to sustain their opposition to the Act. This must be related to the Labour party leadership's decision not to support defiance of the law.

Local autonomy is all very well when it is the discretion of one's own supporters that is at stake, but from the point of view of Wilson, Callaghan and others, the concern was to avoid providing justification for Tory councils refusing to implement Labour legislation in a future parliament.

It is clear that the civil service drew some lessons from its experience with Clay Cross. The Clay Cross councillors were given plenty of opportunities for public defiance, and for high profile media occasions (such as High Court appearances in London). All this sustained their campaign and made law enforcement clumsy and unseemly.

However, the 1980 Housing Act relied on *financial* mechanisms for raising rents, thereby denying opportunities for publicity or open defiance. The regime for local authority housing finance introduced in 1990 uses the same approach and has been highly effective.

Thus, although the Housing Finance Act was defeated by the return of the Labour government in 1974, new means have been devised to give central government greater control over council rents. ■

Notes

1. L Sklair, 'The struggle against the Housing Finance Act', in R Miliband and J Saville (eds) *The Socialist Register 1975*, Merlin Press, London 1975, pp.250-292

2. D Skinner and J Langdon, *The story of Clay Cross*, Spokesman Books, Nottingham, 1974

Peter Malpass is professor of housing policy at the University of the West of England in Bristol

chapter 16

The missing years

Peter Malpass

Between the second world war and the 1970s, housing associations grew to become a diverse group of providers of rented housing

It is customary to identify the origins of modern housing associations in the work of charitable trusts and model dwellings companies in the Victorian period (see chapter two), and housing historians have given plenty of attention (some would say too much[1]) to the activities and achievements of these organisations, but the story has rarely been carried forward much into the 20th century. Meanwhile, writers concerned with housing associations today acknowledge their deep historical roots, but naturally feel under no obligation to reach back beyond the watershed legislation of 1974, which marked the beginning of the modern era for associations. What happened in the missing years?

The term housing association did not come into common usage until the mid 1930s. Until then the generic term 'public utility society' (PUS) was used for bodies registered with the Registrar of Friendly Societies and which adopted rules preventing the payment of interest or dividend at a rate of more than five per cent. PUSs at that time can be divided into three main groups: societies set up on essentially philanthropic lines to provide decent homes for the poor; bodies associated with large industrial undertakings and set up to provide for their employees, and co-partnership societies, set up to provide for subscribing members. The latter was quite successful before 1914 but made little headway thereafter, and never became a mainstream part of the housing association movement.[2] Industrial societies, too, remained rather to one side of the mainstream. There was a further important group composed of charitable trusts which were not registered as friendly societies but which shared their philanthropic aspirations and eligibility for state assistance.

PUSs were eligible for loans from the Public Works Loans Board (PWLB) to cover up to two thirds (later increased to three quarters) of the value of new building. Then, as now, it was necessary to raise the balance from private sources, usually by issuing share capital and loan stock, on which limited interest was paid. Access to PWLB loans gave the societies the advantage of the Board's ability to borrow at low interest rates, but raising the balance could be difficult and undoubtedly reduced the impact made by the societies.

There was no direct subsidy from the Exchequer until the 1919 Housing & Town Planning Act, under which PUSs (but not including those set up by employers to house their own workers) became entitled to assistance which initially covered half the loan charges on approved capital expenditure. From 1923 right through to 1974 housing associations were eligible for the same subsidies as local authorities on new building, although in practice not all of their output was subsidised. The PUSs built 4,545 subsidised houses under the 1919 Act, but in the whole of the inter-war period their total output was only about 50,000[3] – equivalent to the average *annual* production of the local authorities in these years.

During the inter-war years some of the oldest established trusts and societies, including the Society for Improving the Conditions of the Labouring Classes (founded in 1830) and the East End Dwellings Company (1884), concentrated on managing their existing stock and carried out very little development. Occasionally they managed to pull together the funds for limited new build projects. Meanwhile, more recently formed bodies such as the St Pancras House Improvement Society and Liverpool Improved Houses (now Riverside housing association) concentrated on rehabilitating existing property. In areas such as North Kensington, the Octavia Hill system of housing management was kept alive by a group of women managers who worked on a commission basis (usually five per cent of the rents) for several small scale trusts and companies whose main business was rehabilitation of street properties.

Notting Hill housing trust

Before and after: dilapidated terrace in 1960s West London. Notting Hill housing trust was one of a new generation of housing associations formed to deal with such dreadful urban conditions

It was in rehabilitation that PUSs were seen to have most to contribute. In the immediate aftermath of the first world war the emphasis of policy had to be on reducing the overall shortage of housing, but from the late 1920s the focus turned more towards the problem of the poor quality of much of the existing stock. Local authorities had the statutory duty to produce plans for the elimination of slum housing under the 1930 Housing Act, but there was a vocal and well connected lobby arguing for a greater role for PUSs in relation to poor quality houses that were not suitable for demolition. This view was largely endorsed by the committee set up by the government under the chairmanship of Lord Moyne in 1933.[4] The committee recognised that PUSs were concentrated largely in London and that it would be necessary to provide support and supervision as they developed. Accordingly it recommended that there should be a Central Public Utility Council, not unlike the Housing Corporation (which was not established until thirty years later). This body would be responsible for encouraging the formation of new PUSs in areas where they were needed, and for advising the Ministry of Health on loans to PUSs.

However, the local authorities were not generally well disposed to PUSs, seeing in them a danger of unaccountable bodies usurping their rightful role, and in the event the government backed away from legislation to implement the Moyne proposals in full. Instead, the 1935 Housing Act empowered the minister to give financial support to a recognised body representing PUSs and, in a move which pre-figured the growth of stock transfers half a century later, introduced a power for local authorities to hand over to PUSs the management of public housing. The body representing PUSs was the newly formed National Federation of Housing Societies (NFHS), which received an annual grant of £1,000. Some idea of the scale of activity at that time can be obtained from the fact that the initial membership of the NFHS was just 75, although there were believed to be some 226 associations operating in the whole country at that time. Membership rose to 150 by 1939.

Amongst the founder members of the NFHS were some organisations that are still active today, such as the Improved Tenements Association (now part of the Octavia Hill Housing Trust) whose chairman Sir Reginald Rowe was one of the main driving forces behind the creation of the Federation, the Kensington Housing Trust, and, outside London, the Howard Cottage Society, which was set up in 1911 to provide rented housing in the first garden city at Letchworth, Hertfordshire. Long-established charitable trusts such as the Guinness Trust joined within a few years.

The second world war had a serious impact on housing associations in three main ways. First, their concentration in inner London and other big cities meant that they suffered badly from bombing. Second, the re-introduction of blanket rent control in 1939 left them facing rising costs of repair and demands for modernisation with no freedom to raise additional income. And third, the election of a Labour government in July 1945 created a political climate in which the local authorities enjoyed such strong support that the associations found it very difficult to do any new building. The stance of the Labour government towards housing associations was very different from that of the pre-war Tory dominated National government. The attitude was one of reluctant tolerance rather than encouragement, and with local authorities given the role of building for general needs the housing associations were left looking for an appropriate niche.

They found it in building for elderly people. There was a period of growth in the formation of new associations dedicated to providing for elderly people, and established organisations such as the Guinness Trust and the Howard Cottage Society, which had little or no track record in this field, found that it was a way of securing sites, subsidies and the all-important building licences. By 1961 244 members of the NFHS were classified as 'old people's associations', more than were classified as 'general family'.[5] There was a proliferation of associations, and membership of the Federation rose to 651 by 1960, but this was not matched by output, which remained at just a few thousand houses a year throughout the 1950s.

Another relatively successful type of association in the post-war period was the industrial association, set up to provide for workers in specific industries. The British Airways Staff Housing Society (now Airways Housing Society) is a good example, founded in 1946 to build for workers at the recently established Heathrow airport. The Coal Industry Housing Association was expanding rapidly and there were numerous other smaller associations developing up to the mid 1960s, when the government removed their eligibility for subsidy. The role of industry-based associations probably deserves closer attention than it has been given by researchers in the past.

Rent control was lifted from housing associations in 1954, but this made little difference to the rate of new building, given the competition for sites and the generally cool attitude of local authorities. Even big, long established organisations such as the Peabody and Guinness Trusts, each with several thousand dwellings, found it very difficult to carry out new building, partly because they had to devote increasing amounts of spare cash to the modernisation of ageing tenement blocks.

Things began to change when the government introduced measures to stimulate a new kind of housing society. Faced with mounting evidence that the deregulation of private sector rents after 1957 was not leading to renewed investment by landlords, the government introduced an experiment in cost rent and co-ownership housing in the 1961 Housing Act. This was intended to be entirely unsubsidised and aimed at people who were not ready to buy but who would not normally qualify for council housing. Initially a fund of £25 million (plus £3 million for Scotland) was made available to be lent to new style societies, which were expected to be mainly providing cost rent housing. The scheme was to be administered by the NFHS. It was judged to be a success and in the 1964 Housing Act it was re-launched with £100 million, this time administered by the newly created Housing Corporation, which was set up specifically to administer the cost rent and co-ownership scheme and was not then involved in the work of providers of conventional rented housing. The intention was that the Corporation would lend two-thirds of scheme costs, with the balance coming from the building societies.

The initiative required the creation of new societies, some of which budded off from existing associations, and these helped to boost membership of the Federation, which tripled in size during the 1960s. Many of the new societies were formed by groups of architects, solicitors, surveyors and estate agents, who were actively encouraged to apply their expertise to the development of new housing, and were permitted to both sit on management committees and charge fees for professional services rendered. The ethics of this were later questioned, especially when large amounts of public subsidy became available, and in due course it was prohibited.

In the event, only some 1,600 dwellings were built by cost rent societies and co-ownership emerged as the dominant form, producing a total of over 35,000, but only after clarification of co-owners' entitlement to mortgage interest tax relief on the interest portion of the 'rent' and, from 1967, the introduction of the option mortgage subsidy. So the idea of new forms of unsubsidised housing did not come to much, and by the early 1980s virtually all of the co-ownership dwellings had been converted into conventional owner-occupation. However, what did come out of this episode was a number of organisations which later became highly successful mainstream housing associations, including North British, Sanctuary, Orbit and Knightstone.

In parallel with the cost rent and co-ownership initiative there was a new burst of energy directed mainly at the rehabilitation of houses in run-down areas of large cities, especially London. At that time, less than twenty years after the war, slum clearance was beginning to have an impact on established communities, and there was still a huge amount of decaying privately rented housing, lacking in basic amenities. There were also increasing numbers of newly arrived households of various kinds, who were often not eligible for council housing and not welcomed by the old charitable trusts. In this situation a number of activists began to organise new housing associations, committed to maintaining a sense of local community by renovation rather than redevelopment. Particular success was achieved in the mid-1960s by the newly formed Notting Hill Housing Trust and Paddington Churches Housing Association.

The churches played an important part in the promotion of housing associations in the 1960s. In 1964 the British Churches Housing Trust was set up to promote the formation of new associations to work in a wide field and across the country. 34 new associations emerged from or were supported by the Trust, including Richmond Churches, Bristol Churches and Coventry Churches (now part of Touchstone). Another group of associations was promoted by the Catholic Housing Aid Society, and these included Family and South London Family.

In 1966 a group of organisations, mostly church based, came together to form Shelter, the national campaign for the homeless. Shelter's main role at that time was to raise funds for the promotion and support of housing associations, and some £3 million was raised in the years before Housing Corporation funding was extended in 1974. Shelter funds were used to help established associations and to assist in the formation of new ones, mainly by helping to meet the cost of staff salaries. Among those that received help were Notting Hill Housing Trust, Circle 33, Liverpool Improved Houses, and Copec (now Focus).

The work of housing associations in the 1960s was further boosted by a growing willingness by local authorities to provide assistance in the form of loans for the purchase and renovation of old properties. The Greater London Council, in particular, supported a programme of about 10,000 dwellings per year by the early 1970s. The availability of loans secured against properties whose value could be relied upon to rise meant that it was relatively easy to build up a substantial operation from a small beginning.

Associations also had access to improvement grants, and the 1967 Housing Subsidies Act introduced a subsidy to cover a proportion of the loan charges incurred by associations in acquiring property for improvement. This was extended in the 1969 Housing Act. The 1972 Housing Finance Act proposed a completely new subsidy system for both local authorities and housing associations. The new system was to be based on 'fair rents' and a reducing level of subsidy. This was seen as creating serious problems for associations, who would face the prospect of falling subsidy income with no freedom under the fair rents regime to raise rents to meet any budget shortfall. The system's deficiencies were quickly recognised and the government moved towards a quite different approach, based not on annual revenue subsidy but a one-off grant towards approved capital costs. This became the Housing Association Grant (HAG) introduced in the 1974 Housing Act, and together with the re-launching of the Housing Corporation as the regulatory and funding body for all types of housing association it marked the beginning of an entirely new era in state support for voluntary housing.

Some people like to refer to the housing association *movement*, implying a shared sense of purpose and direction, but the diversity of organisations has always meant that the differences were at least as important as any shared values. Certainly in the 1960s there was a quite marked division between the newly emergent Shelter-backed associations, mostly concentrating on rehabilitation, and the cost rent and co-ownership societies which carried out new building. Whereas the former were concerned with communities and with people in urgent housing need, the latter were seen to be more commercial and to cater for a quite different type of household. The old charitable trusts and associations tended to be seen by the new activists as generally moribund and out of touch with the needs of the time.

In the days before Housing Corporation registration and regulation there was much more diversity amongst associations than there is now. This was partly because, in the absence of a standard framework, each association tended to reflect the influence and interests of the individuals involved in setting it up. But it was also due to the vitality created by the ease with which a group of concerned individuals could get together and form a new association. Unlike local authorities, where change had to be produced from within existing structures, old associations which had become rigid and outdated could simply be by-passed and ignored. This must have contributed to the dynamism and variety within the movement over the years.

The 1974 Act undoubtedly launched housing associations as

mainstream providers of affordable rented housing, rescuing them from the margins of the housing system, but the price that they paid was some loss of autonomy. It marks the start of the modern era for housing associations.

It is tempting to believe that, although some associations can claim deep historical roots, all the action has been concentrated into the last 25 years, particularly the momentous changes in association activity since 1988 (see chapter 20). This chapter has shown that in fact there is an important story to be told about the transformation of voluntary housing from its Victorian origins to the present day. It must also be acknowledged, however, that the pace of change has been greater since 1974, and in particular since 1988, than in the whole of the century leading up to that point. ■

Notes

1. M Daunton, *House and home in the Victorian city*, E Arnold, 1983, p1
2. J Birchall, 'Co-partnership housing and the garden city movement', *Planning Perspectives*, vol. 10, 1995 pp329-358
3. *The operations of housing associations*, report by the housing management and housing associations sub-committee of the central housing advisory committee, Ministry of Health, 1939, p.4
4. P Garside, 'Central government, local authorities and the voluntary housing sector 1919-1939' in A O'Day (ed) *Government and institutions in the post-1832 UK*, Mellon Press, 1995
5. NFHS *Annual Report 1961/62*, p.5

Peter Malpass is professor of housing policy at the University of the West of England in Bristol

chapter 17

Changing duties

Janet Richards and John Goodwin

A private member's bill in 1977 was the turning point that gave homeless people the basic right to be housed by councils

The 1977 Housing (Homeless Persons) Act was a landmark in British housing policy. It placed the first ever duties on housing authorities to help homeless people and established homelessness as an integral part of the housing function.

Both the Poor Law and the 1948 National Assistance Act treated homelessness as a 'welfare' problem. Under the Poor Law, homeless people could get shelter in the workhouse, provided they had a right to settle in the district. They were typically regarded as undeserving and feckless, and workhouse conditions were harsh and punitive. The legacy of this regime had a lasting influence on attitudes towards homeless people, and policies to help them.

The 1948 Act abolished the Poor Law and section 21(1)(b) put a duty on county authorities to provide temporary accommodation for those in urgent, or unforeseen need. Ministry of Health circular 87/48 stressed that the purpose was to assist people made homeless through an emergency such as fire or flood; it was not intended to deal with the 'inadequately housed'.

Welfare and social services departments, which assumed the duty, tended to interpret the Act as a hostel and casework service, with the result that deterrent Poor Law practices lived on. Conditions in temporary accommodation were usually inadequate and often in former Poor Law institutions. Communal facilities, sex segregation and time limits on stay were common.

Families were frequently split up. Some hostels would not

SAYS 'FACE THE F...TS

Shelter

Shelter's first director, Des Wilson, campaigning in the 1960s: Shelter was a member of the Joint Charities Group whose campaign in the 1970s led to the 1977 Housing (Homeless Persons) Act. The charity mounted a new campaign in 1994 when the government proposed to repeal the Act. Although the campaign received wide support, the homelessness law was replaced by the more restrictive 1996 Housing Act

permit men, and children were sometimes taken into care, leaving the parents to find their own accommodation. In 1974/75, 2,800 children in England and Wales ended up in care solely because of homelessness.

Many authorities applied eligibility criteria, for example by refusing to help pregnant women until after the birth. They also typically refused to accommodate people who had previously lived outside the area, which led to families being shuttled between authorities, with neither accepting responsibility. Differences in local authority practices meant that geography played a large part in determining the chances of getting help.

The 1948 Act was unable to cope with the scale and nature of post-war homelessness. The number of homeless people seeking help grew every year, and the majority were not victims of an emergency, but of the housing shortage. They needed permanent homes, which welfare departments, with no housing stock, were unable to provide.

The central weakness of the Act was that it treated homelessness as a welfare matter and gave duties to the ministry of health (later the DHSS) and social services authorities, when homelessness was a housing problem. Housing departments were usually unwilling to house homeless people, as they were seen as undeserving and irresponsible. To house the homeless was considered contrary to waiting list principles. Co-operation between welfare and housing departments was poor, and hindered by the fact that in most parts of the country they were in different tiers of local government.

This split responsibility left a policy vacuum in which, for nearly 30 years, neither ministry took decisive action to change the legal framework. The ministry of health was even reluctant to use its default powers to enforce the law. The ministry of housing's *laissez-faire* approach to housing authorities precluded it from interfering in their rehousing policies. So homelessness was a subject 'on which government expressed concern, commissioned research, set up working parties and issued guidance and advisory circulars, but did not legislate'.[1] Moreover, any advice that was issued was largely ignored by local authorities.

For example, the Central Housing Advisory Committee's 1955 report *Unsatisfactory tenants* advocated that housing departments be responsible for housing homeless people, as did joint MOH/MHLG circular 4/59 the 1968 Cullingworth report *Council housing, purposes, procedures and priorities*; and the 1968 Seebohm report on local authority personal social services. This conclusion was reiterated by the DHSS-commissioned Greve report (1971) on homelessness in London, and both this and research by Glastonbury (1971) for another DHSS inquiry, clearly showed the 1948 Act to be ineffective.

Throughout the 1960s and early 1970s the case for reform mounted. Academic research demonstrated that homelessness was primarily caused by housing shortage rather than by personal inadequacy. Voluntary groups and charities publicised the problem and there was growing public concern and media interest in the plight of homeless families, particularly after the screening in November 1966 of *Cathy come home*, a BBC television drama which showed the plight of a homeless woman.

Yet, despite evidence that the 1948 Act was not working and

homelessness was in fact increasing, the 1972 Local Government Act reduced the duty to provide temporary accommodation to a discretionary power, with effect from April 1974.

This prompted Shelter, the Catholic Housing Aid Society, the Campaign for the Homeless and Rootless (CHAR), SHAC and the Child Poverty Action Group to form the Joint Charities Group (JCG) with the aim of seeking amendments to the 1974 Local Government Bill to restore the statutory duty and impose it on housing authorities. Although the amendments were unsuccessful, the campaign led to a DHSS directive, reinstating the duty, and secured an opposition pledge that a Labour government would bring in laws imposing the duty. Over the next two and a half years, the JCG pressed for legislation to give housing authorities statutory responsibility for homelessness.

In February 1974, the Conservative government responded to the many reports calling for a duty on housing authorities with a joint DoE/Department of Health/Welsh Office circular 18/74, which took effect at the same time as local government reorganisation. This circular later proved significant in forming the blueprint for the Homeless Persons Bill and the Code of Guidance. It acknowledged that homelessness was an 'extreme form of housing need' and recommended that housing authorities take over homelessness duties from social services. The circular also introduced the concept of priority groups. It advocated that where the housing situation was particularly difficult, authorities should give priority to families with dependent children and to single people made homeless through emergency, or who were vulnerable because of old age, disability, pregnancy or other special reasons.

There was now a clear anomaly in government policy: the statutory duty to assist the homeless lay with social services authorities, but government was advising housing authorities to take on the task.

A Labour government was returned in the general election of February 1974, but despite pre-election pledges, homelessness legislation was not among its priorities. The following year it initiated a review of homelessness, but its consultation document said that the government was not convinced that new legislation was appropriate.

A DoE survey into the implementation of circular 18/74, carried out for the review, revealed that by April 1975 most authorities had not adopted the priority group criteria and only a third of housing departments had accepted sole responsibility for the homeless. In some areas, neither housing nor social services would accept responsibility, with the result that families were shunted backwards and forwards.

By late October 1975, the government concluded that legislation was necessary after all. Homelessness was a growing political embarrassment. In 1976, around 33,700 households were accepted by authorities in England – more than double the number in 1971. Faced with pressure from all sides for legal reform, and with DoE research supporting this view, it was clear that circular 18/74 would only be implemented if it had the force of the law.

In Spring 1976 the DoE began separate, but parallel, consultation meetings with the local authority associations (LAAs) and the JCG to consider proposals for legislation. The JCG played an influential role in the consultation process, as DoE officials relied on its advice and support in resisting local government pressure for a limited duty.

The government's lack of commitment to the legislation became apparent when it dropped the Homeless Persons Bill from the 1976 Queen's Speech, ostensibly because of insufficient parliamentary time. However, it indicated that it would support a Private Member's Bill on the subject. Fortunately the Liberal housing spokesman, Stephen Ross MP, came fourth in the private members' ballot and agreed to adopt a Bill prepared by the JCG, but was permitted to use the DoE's own Bill, which was better drafted.

Although the Bill had government backing and sponsors from all parties, its prospects of becoming law were threatened by the government's slender majority, and it was at risk of not surviving the parliamentary session.

The Lib-Lab pact in the Spring of 1977 brought some relief on this front, and was instrumental in securing more parliamentary time for the Bill. But even so, a safe passage was not assured, because the Bill did not reach Standing Committee until mid-June and had to complete its stages by the end of July.

The objective of the Bill in its original form was to give legislative power to circular 18/74. It provided a statutory definition of homelessness and gave housing authorities duties to secure accommodation for people in priority need and to advise and assist others. The Bill reflected the JCG's position except that it also wanted a statutory right of appeal, default powers for the secretary of state, the extension of priority need to cover single people, and a requirement that the accommodation provided be reasonably suitable for the person's needs.

The Association of County Councils (ACC) was largely in favour of the provisions, but the Association of District Councils (ADC) and the Association of Metropolitan Authorities (AMA) were concerned about the cost of implementation and the loss of local autonomy. They did not want a legal definition of homelessness, or a statutory right to housing, but preferred a general duty on housing authorities to give homeless people advice and help to secure accommodation.

The ADC and the JCG emerged as the dominant opposing lobbies; the JCG briefed Stephen Ross while the ADC's case was fought by Conservative MP Hugh Rossi and fellow backbenchers.

The Bill's opponents argued that it would be unfair to applicants on the waiting list; would result in people deliberately making themselves homeless; would swamp authorities in desirable areas, such as seaside resorts, which they claimed would attract influxes of homeless people and would restrict local discretion. They vilified the Bill in parliamentary debates as a charter for 'queue-jumpers', 'rent-dodgers', 'scroungers and scrimshankers.'

The opposition succeeded in weakening the Bill through amendments which said that people deemed intentionally homeless were not entitled to accommodation, limiting the authority's obligations only to people with a local connection, and defining priority need and vulnerability in vague terms.

These concessions were made to avoid delays that would have killed the Bill. The ADC and AMA counter campaign also carried weight, because its members would have the job of implementing the new law and their co-operation was vital if the Act was to work.

So the 1977 Housing (Homeless Persons) Act was a compromise measure. It was less liberal than circular 18/74, and legitimised the continuation of practices which limited help to local people, and discriminated between the 'deserving' and the 'undeserving'.

Nevertheless, it was an achievement in securing basic rights for homeless people, and was the first significant attempt by government to tell councils whom they should house. The JCG hoped that it would be the first step towards more comprehensive duties to all homeless people.

The legislation was later consolidated in the 1985 Housing Act and the 1987 Housing (Scotland) Act, and in 1988 the main provisions were extended for the first time to Northern Ireland by the Housing (Northern Ireland) Order 1988 No 1990 (NI23).

The Act required housing authorities to provide advice and assistance to homeless people and to secure accommodation for those in priority need, who were unintentionally homeless. Priority need was defined as pregnancy, having dependent children, being vulnerable because of old age, mental illness or handicap, or physical disability or other special reason, and being homeless or threatened with homelessness as a result of an emergency such as flood or fire.

Authorities were required to have regard to the accompanying Code of Guidance, giving advice on interpretation and good practice, but were not obliged to follow it. The Code reflected some of the spirit of the original Bill in advocating a wider interpretation of the authority's duties than that laid down in the Act.

The number of households accepted as homeless under the Act rose steadily for many years. DoE figures record increases in England from 53,110 in 1978 to a peak of 142,890 in 1992, declining to 116,870 in 1996. The law primarily benefited families with children, who formed the majority of acceptances.

The two main reasons for acceptance as homeless under the Act were the breakdown of sharing arrangements with relatives and friends, and breakdown of a relationship with a partner. This pattern changed little over the years, except that mortgage default grew in significance from the late 1980s. However, the pattern was different in pre-Act days, when eviction by private landlords and rent arrears were major causes of homelessness.

The Act largely curtailed bad practices such as splitting families and taking children into care. The local connection rules and the LAAs' *Agreement on procedures for referral of the homeless* reduced the incidence of inter-authority disputes over responsibility. Fears that the Act would lead to homeless people converging on popular areas proved unfounded – DoE figures show that most households accepted as homeless were resident in the area one year previously.

However, the Act had certain gaps and flaws: the duty to secure accommodation did not extend to non-vulnerable single adults and young people, so it did little to relieve the growing problem of homelessness among these groups. The definition of homelessness did not encompass homelessness resulting from violence from persons outside the home, or racial and sexual harassment. Applicants had no right of appeal, so could only challenge decisions through judicial review in the high court on grounds that the authority had acted contrary to the principles of administrative law.

With no statutory right of appeal, no default procedures and a Code of Guidance that had no statutory force, differences in interpretation and implementation were inevitable, resulting in marked local variations in rates of acceptance and findings of intentional homelessness.

For example, a DoE survey in 1986 found that having rent arrears and moving to an area to seek work were regarded as 'intentional homelessness' by 45 per cent and 55 per cent of authorities respectively, while 40 per cent of authorities did not accept children leaving care as homeless.[2]

An Audit Commission report in 1989 identified similar discrepancies in policy and procedures and highlighted the need to improve performance.[3] But it also acknowledged that many homeless persons units operated under extreme pressure and needed higher levels of investment in order to cope with demand.

The homelessness duties in the Act were never backed by adequate resources for housing authorities, which operated in a period of deepening housing crisis. The decline of the private rented sector, the sale of council houses, and successive cuts in housing investment and new building in the 1980s created a growing shortage of affordable housing. Councils were left to deal with increasing numbers of homeless people, while having fewer properties in which to rehouse them.

As a result, homeless people accepted under the Act received a growing share of council lettings – in England the proportion increased from 14 per cent in 1978/79 to 30 per cent in 1989/90, and in London from 25 per cent to 59 per cent over the same period (DoE HIP figures).

The Audit Commission study showed that most homeless applicants were already on local authority waiting lists, but nevertheless, the notion that homeless people were 'queue-jumpers' took hold and fuelled calls for new and more restrictive legislation.

In 1988 the Conservative government initiated a review of homelessness legislation, prompting fears that the statutory duties would be dismantled.[4] Both the voluntary sector and the local authority associations (with the exception of the ADC) urged that the law be left intact.

In 1989 the review concluded that the law should remain unchanged. It found that, 'the legislation has worked reasonably well and should remain in place as a "long stop" to help those who through no fault of their own have become homeless.' The government did however decide to review the local connection rules in order 'to moderate undue demands on the most heavily burdened areas', and to review the Code of Guidance 'to help secure greater consistency between authorities.' A new Scottish Code was published in May 1991, followed in August by a revised Code for England and Wales. Both took a generally more liberal approach. They gave extensive guidance on the prevention of homelessness, emphasised the need for performance monitoring, and suggested performance targets for processing homelessness applications.

Against this background, the announcement by housing minister Sir George Young at the 1993 Conservative party conference that there was to be another full scale review of the homelessness legislation would appear surprising. But the announcement was not wholly unexpected given the political context of the early 1990s, which included the Conservatives' 'back to basics' campaign and speeches attacking single mothers. The homelessness legislation was wrongly portrayed as giving special priority to single parents at the expense of couples who were patiently waiting to be re-housed before starting a family.

The government published its proposals for changing the legislation in a Green Paper in January 1994.[5] The proposals were far more restrictive than most housing professionals and campaigners had expected. The Green Paper sought to restrict the legal definition of homelessness, remove the rights of homeless people to permanent housing, and refer homeless people to the private rented sector. It was explicit about the government's intention to deal with the high level of homelessness by redefining demand, rather than increasing the supply of decent, affordable, rented housing: 'While the number of statutorily homeless households has shown a welcome decline...the underlying trend could continue upward unless steps are taken to alter the current legislation.'

The Green Paper claimed that homelessness had become a 'fast track' into social housing. In fact 77 per cent of new local authority lettings were, at the time, going to people already on waiting lists.

A campaign was mounted by Shelter, the LAAs and other organisations to defend the existing legislation, despite its defects. The 10,000 responses to the government's consultation were overwhelmingly negative and there was speculation that the plans would be dropped. However, reform of the homelessness legislation was included in the broad housing White Paper *Our future homes: opportunity, choice, responsibility* in June 1995.

After publication of the housing Bill in January 1996 some concessions were made to the housing lobby. For example, the new duty to temporarily accommodate unintentionally homeless people was extended from 12 months to two years. But the main planks of the reforms remained intact and became law as Part VII of the 1996 Housing Act.

The 1996 Act repealed Part III of the 1985 Housing Act, putting an end to the legislation which had provided a safety net for over four million people since 1977.

The new homelessness law took effect on 20 January 1997, less than four months before the Conservative government lost power. The new Act bore some similarities to its predecessor, for example the categories of people in 'priority need' remained unchanged, but it also contained significant changes:

- Many people from abroad were no longer eligible for assistance
- Local authorities did not have a duty to house homeless people if suitable accommodation (such as private rented housing) was available in the area
- The duty to secure accommodation was limited to two years
- Local authorities were given a new duty to make advice and

information about homelessness, and how to prevent it, available to all people in their area.

This new framework was closely linked to the new law on the allocation of social housing by local authorities in Part VI of the Act, introduced on 1 April 1997. The new system required every authority to maintain a housing register, but only 'qualifying persons' were allowed to be placed on it – excluding many people from abroad. Homeless people were allowed to join the register, but were no longer to be given 'reasonable preference' in the allocation of tenancies – a right which they had enjoyed under the earlier legislation.

The overall effect of these changes was to give homeless people a much lower chance of obtaining long term housing from local authorities and housing associations. In areas with viable private rented sectors, private landlords were expected to play a much larger role in housing homeless people. However, this was often not a realistic option given the high levels of rents, restrictions on housing benefit and the reluctance of many landlords to house people with children or who were vulnerable – the very people who qualified for help under the legislation.

The Labour party opposed the changes to the homelessness law and promised, should they win power, to: 'restore a clear, strong framework based on the principles of the 1977 Act, which will require local authorities to secure permanent accommodation for homeless people in priority need'.[6]

Labour's election victory in May 1997 did bring early promise of reform, though not the full restoration of the 1977 framework that some had hoped for. With many competing priorities, new primary homelessness legislation was not included in the Queen's Speech, but housing minister Hilary Armstrong did announce that significant changes to the regulations would be made. Unintentionally homeless people who had a priority need would have their 'reasonable preference' in the allocation of tenancies by local authorities restored from November 1997, and, from September 1997, accommodation for homeless people in the private sector would only be regarded as suitable if it was available for two years.

It remains to be seen what further changes, if any, the Labour government will make to homelessness law. But unless the shortage of affordable housing is also tackled, what remains of the legal safety net will continue to be strained. ∎

Notes

1. N Raynsford 'The Housing (Homeless Persons) Act 1977' in N Deakin (ed), *Policy change in government*, RIPA 1986
2. A Evans and S Duncan, *Responding to homelessness: local authority policy and practice*, HMSO 1988
3. Audit Commission, *Housing the homeless: the local authority role*, HMSO 1989
4. 'The government's review of homelessness legislation', HMSO 1989
5. Department of the Environment, *Access to local authority and housing association tenancies*, HMSO 1994
6. N Raynsford, ROOF debate, 1996

Janet Richards is manager of the Chartered Institute of Housing's Good Practice Unit. John Goodwin is deputy editor of ROOF

The big sell-off

Ray Forrest and Alan Murie

Housing policy has been reshaped by the sale and transfer of over two million council homes since 1980

Selling council houses was the most substantial element in the privatisation policies of the Conservative governments between 1979 and 1997 and was a privatisation which benefited ordinary working families rather than the wealthy or those with capacity to shift their investment portfolios around. Over those years some 2.3 million public sector dwellings have been sold to home owners and a further 250,000 through stock transfers. Most of these sales have been under the right to buy introduced in the 1980 Housing Act.

Those who bought have mostly bought good houses at cheap (discounted) prices, and in general they have benefited from house price inflation. In some cases, they have bought because it is cheaper to buy than to rent. Rising interest rates have probably had less impact on those who bought under right to buy than on those who bought at market prices elsewhere. However, the impact of recessions and job losses was felt by this group as much as any other.

Evaluating council house sales and other stock transfers over 17 years is complex. The policy has not operated in a vacuum. It has formed part of a general reshaping of housing policy. The council sector has not changed only because of sales. It was already changing in important ways through the long-established decline of private renting, the privileged treatment of home ownership and social, economic and demographic change. There is no simple cause and effect between selling council houses and what has happened to the public sector. Most obviously, the effect of council house sales would have been very different had a major public sector building programme been taking place at the same time. It is important, therefore, to consider sales, not just in terms of who has benefited and what has been sold, but in terms of the indirect and longer-term changes which will flow from sales and in terms of their role in the broader policy context.

Selling council houses is not a new policy. Significant sales have been completed at various stages and legislation has consistently included powers for sale with ministerial consent. In the post-war period, refusals to countenance such sales gave way to a general consent to sales in 1951. There followed a period of fluctuating central government encouragement for sales, and different responses at a local level.

The 1980 Housing Act changed the formula. The power to sell with approval from the secretary of state continued but, for most council dwellings, a right to buy was also introduced.

This and subsequent legislation involved three key elements:

● Council tenants were given a right to buy
● Substantial discounts were given, linked to length of tenancy and applied to a market valuation
● Council tenants were given a right to a mortgage from their local authority.

Through the 1980s, discounts were raised progressively to encourage further sales. By 1986, maximum discounts on houses stood at 60 per cent after 30 years' tenancy. Those in flats qualified for 70 per cent after 15 years. The original justification for discounting prices for council house sales (prior to the right to buy) derived from the lower value of properties in the private rented sector with sitting tenants as opposed to vacant possession. The link to length of tenancy came later, and the discount rate became no more than a balancing act between providing sufficient incentive to maintain sales and generating a certain level of capital receipts. Substantial discounts and the right to buy have been backed up by major publicity campaigns, rising rents and changes of landlord as factors encouraging purchase.

As the right to buy progressed, new elements were added to the privatisation package. The 1988 Housing Act was notable for facilitating new forms of housing privatisation. The most important element was the provision of a choice of landlord for all council tenants. These 'tenants' choice' arrangements set out procedures,

Press Association

Lucky buyers: An Essex family celebrate their right to buy with a visit from Margaret Thatcher

including ballots, through which tenants could set in motion a change of landlord and express dissatisfaction with their municipal landlord by moving to another registered landlord (usually a housing association). In practice this part of the 1988 legislation proved ineffective. Tenants chose not to transfer except in a small number of cases. A second element in the 1988 legislation – housing action trusts (HATs) – also proved ineffective. Some HATs were set up later on, but only after legal change allowed the HATs to be strongly influenced by local authorities. Again, tenants resisted attempts to replace local authority control, except where this was supported by the local authorities themselves. The major new element in the privatisation package was 'large-scale voluntary transfer (LSVT). These transfers of housing stock involved a similar procedure to that set out for tenants' choice, but were initiated by the local authority rather than by tenants. By the end of 1993 tenants' choice had not resulted in the transfer of a single property, but transfers had taken place under parallel arrangements for landlord-initiated LSVTs. Some 23 transfers had been completed and these

Built to Last?

- Fewer economically active
- Fewer multiple earner households
- Fewer higher income households
- Declining level of car ownership
- More households with no earners
- Declining role as family housing
- Increase in female headed households
- Increase in unskilled manual workers
- More elderly people
- Ageing dwelling stock
- Declining proportion of 3-4 bedroomed houses
- Increasing proportion of flats
- Increasing proportion of lettings to the homeless
- Increasing proportion of tenants on state benefits

involved the total stock of these councils – around a quarter of a million dwellings had been transferred by mid-1997. Nevertheless, the right to buy continues to dominate – accounting for well over 80 per cent of all transfers since 1979.

In 1979, 32 per cent of all households in Great Britain were in council housing. By 1995 the comparable figure was 19 per cent. This decline cannot be attributed to council house sales in isolation. High sales have coincided with low and falling levels of public sector new build. Between 1980 and 1981, sales of local authority dwellings in England and Wales outstripped public sector new build for the first time, and have done so by a wide margin ever since. In previous periods of high discretionary sales, new building was considerably higher than disposals.

Sales peaked in 1982, and began to decline steadily, prompting some commentators to suggest that the future impact would be limited. By the end of the 1980s, however, sales had risen again to the second highest level of all time. They fell back substantially in 1990 and have subsequently levelled out at 60-70,000. Although much lower than previous years, this figure is higher than in any year before 1980 and much higher than the rate of new building.

Against a background of high house prices (and therefore high sales valuations), rising interest rates and a general recession in the owner-occupied market, the high levels of council house sales in 1988 and 1989 may seem surprising. This needs to be balanced, however, against the impact of rising real incomes for households in employment, lower levels of unemployment and rising rents.

Moreover, high discounts cushion right to buy purchasers to some degree from rising prices and mortgage interest rates. The uncertain future for council tenants associated with various provisions in the 1988 Housing Act and the 1989 Local Government Act may also have acted as a further incentive to leave the sector. The fall-off in sales in 1990 reflects the generally depressed state of the property market at that time combined with rising unemployment, particularly in areas where sales had traditionally been high. Into the 1990s sales continued to reflect the state of the home ownership market and the changing stock of council houses.

The right to buy is normally associated with the decline of council housing. But the other side of the equation is equally important. There has been a cumulative impact on the home ownership sector. Without council house sales, the substantial expansion of home ownership throughout the 1980s would not have been achieved. In the early 1980s, sales added more to home ownership than new private sector building. Around every tenth dwelling in the home ownership sector in Britain is now a former local authority property. And between 1981 and 1991 tenure transfers from the council to the home ownership sector accounted for 46 per cent of the growth of home ownership – a growth from 55 to 68 per cent of all households. What is less clear and will remain an important policy issue well into the next century is the market impact of such a major addition to the private sector. The concentration of sitting tenant purchasers in the middle to late middle age stages of the family life cycle means that there will be an inevitable bulge of resales of former council properties. These are likely to gather momentum around 2010.

The resale of former council dwellings has in the main been relatively unproblematic. As it was the best dwellings which were sold in the early stages of the right to buy, the first wave of resales has generally consisted of the most desirable properties. Their saleability, like all properties, has varied with market conditions, although former council-owned properties have represented good value for money. What is clear is that there has not been a rush to sell after any period of discount repayment has elapsed. This reflects the age profile of purchasers and their satisfaction with the dwellings they bought and the neighbourhoods in which they live.

Different issues have, however, arisen with the sale of flats which gathered pace in the late 1980s as a result of higher discounts, a booming market and a more competitive mortgage market. Not all purpose-built flats in the public rental stock in England are problematic in terms of maintenance, repair or saleability. But the most extreme contrasts are probably to be found between the high quality houses in the inner and outer suburbs and the high rise, system-built tower blocks in inner city locations or on peripheral estates. Few of those properties have been sold, but where sales have occurred difficulties tend to have arisen. Some of these problems were associated with the generally depressed state of the housing market in Britain in the 1989 to 1996 period. Some are, however, associated with the basic design of the dwellings and their production and management histories in the public sector.

These are properties which were designed to be managed on a collective basis. When a single property is sold to a tenant, complex and often imprecise calculations are required to apportion responsibility and financial liability for repairs and maintenance. The apportionment of costs has to cover a proportion of the general management costs for the landlord, routine maintenance and repair, cleaning and maintenance of common areas such as hallways and open spaces, lift maintenance and replacement, capital works associated with roofs and windows, charges for communal heating systems and so forth. All of these charges are open to challenge from leaseholders. All require detailed justification by the authority. And, most fundamentally, some justifiable charges have proved unaffordable.

Moreover, as the right to buy progressed and flat sales gathered pace, government was producing another set of policies encouraging local authorities to cost their various functions more precisely and to recover costs as fully as possible where appropriate. Those who had bought public sector flats were progressively exposed to a new regime where local authority service charges were increasing and where the justification for such charges was more transparent. This produced well

Table 1: Regional pattern of council house sales 1979-93		
Year	% of stock	% of England sales
North (excl. Cumbria)	25.6	8
Yorks and Humberside	23.9	9
East Midlands	28.8	8
Eastern	38.0	5
South East (incl. Gtr London)	28.2	17
South East (excl. Gtr London)	39.9	24
South West	33.3	8
West Midlands	25.9	11
North West (incl. Cumbria)	22.9	10
England	29.4	
Scotland	24.8	
Wales	31.0	
Source: CSO (1995) Regional Trends 30		

publicised situations where purchasers of flats were on occasion presented with bills for capital works which exceeded the current value of their properties. Rising service charges at a time of falling property values proved to be a recipe for conflict and discontent.

Another important dimension of the right to buy concerns the value of the assets which are being acquired by individual households. Council house purchasers were to become members of the emerging 'inheritance' economy, with housing equity to pass on to their children and grandchildren. The geographical unevenness of property values has meant, inevitably, that some people have gained considerably more than others. Sales have been highest in areas of high and appreciating property values. In those areas discounts have been worth most and have been a major incentive to buy. By way of contrast, fewer have bought in the north of the country. There, purchasers have paid less, their discount was worth less, and absolute increases in property values since purchase have been least. In other words, the generally less affluent North has benefited less than the generally more affluent South.

When the right to buy was introduced in 1980 there was at least an implicit assumption that the level of sales would be fairly uniform

Built to Last?

across the country. Although the demand for home ownership shows slight regional variations, these were not sufficient to suggest that there would be substantial differences in the take up of the opportunity to buy council houses. It was also assumed that in the absence of any political obstruction, pent-up demand for home ownership would be released everywhere. In practice, however, the pattern has been very different. For England as a whole between 1979 and 1993 some 29 per cent of the council stock was sold (Table 1). Throughout the period sales continued to be highest in the south and east of England. Moreover there was little evidence of the slowest sellers catching up. For example, between 1985 and 1990 the percentage of stock sold rose by the greatest number of percentage points in the Eastern region (15 per cent), the South East (17 per cent), South West (13 per cent) and East Midlands (17 per cent). It rose by the smallest amount in the North West (eight per cent). Lower sales in parts of Greater London complicates any simple North-South pattern but in general, rather than smoothing out the regional tenure structure of Britain, sales have contributed to a greater unevenness.

At local authority level sales have been most significant in the more prosperous urban and rural districts where council housing and renting was already limited; where home ownership was already well established; where houses rather than flats predominated in the council stock; and where incomes and employment were generally high. The lowest sales have been in large urban authorities, in particular in inner London and the North West of England. Rates of sale vary from 65 per cent in Mid Bedfordshire to 9.5 per cent in Hackney.

Who buys council houses? The picture is now well-established and has not changed significantly over the years. Studies in different regions and localities show a similar pattern related to age, household structure and occupation. Put simply, buyers have been drawn disproportionately from households in work, in the middle of the family life cycle, with one or more earners, with two or more adults and in white collar, skilled or semi-skilled occupations. Put negatively, those who do not buy are the youngest and oldest, the unemployed, female-headed households, lone parent families, and those in the lowest paid and unskilled sectors. And in most areas, there is a coincidence between those groups with least bargaining power in the labour market and those in the least desirable parts of the council stock – flats and maisonettes and houses on the least popular estates. Those households have least incentive to buy, and least resources to do so.

The development of council house sales policy has not been universally welcomed. The discretionary policies which applied before 1980 were adopted by some Labour local authorities, and were rejected by some Conservative ones. Much of the early controversy about the policy related to the Labour party's opposition, and to what government regarded as obstructive, delaying tactics by some local authorities.

Government's response was not only to tighten legislation, but also to use its powers to pressurise and intervene. Legal challenges to this failed, and the degree of central scrutiny and promotion of policy implementation has been in stark contrast to, say, its approach to homelessness. If this opposition was unsuccessful, that of housing associations was more effective. Government's plans to extend the policy in this area and in relation to dwellings used by elderly and disabled persons were repeatedly thwarted, especially by the House of Lords.

But the controversies about sales are not all about resistance. The degree of centralisation of policy has itself been questioned. The private sector housing industry and housing professions have generally benefited. And the activities of some private sector agencies seeking to generate business through the sales policy have raised controversy. The manipulation of discretionary policies, vacant sales and allocations, notably in Westminster and Wandsworth, have been very widely questioned.

The importance of the right to buy and other dwelling sales in government public expenditure plans has been apparent ever since 1979. Capital receipts from the housing programme have been more important than the headline-catching sales of state-owned enterprises.

Only from 1984/85 onwards have non-housing capital receipts exceeded housing receipts in any one year. For the period 1979/89 capital receipts for the housing programme were £17.5 billion compared with £23.4 billion from all other privatisations. In this period housing receipts represented 43 per cent of all privatisation proceeds. Just as important, they provided a continuing stream of receipts rather than a short-lived windfall and have been an important element in public expenditure planning. Sales of public sector dwellings in Britain since 1979 have generated almost £27 billion (see table 2). The implications for taxation and borrowing of any given level of expenditure are reduced if there are capital receipts against which this can be offset. The housing programme made a considerable contribution to reductions in the overall public sector borrowing requirement (PSBR) and to public sector debt repayment.

Perhaps most critically under the Conservative governments the large receipts accruing to the housing programme were not used to boost housing investment. This is more evident if we refer only to local authority and new town investment in new building acquisitions and renovation of their stock, i.e. to the investment programme for public sector housing, and compare this with capital receipts from the sale of public sector housing. In England in 1979/80 investment in these areas was £2,052 million, while receipts were £491 million. At the peak of capital receipts in England (1989/90) the equivalent cash figures for investment were £3,276 million and for receipts £2,774 million. Net investment in these terms (by local authorities and new towns in the provision of public sector housing) had fallen from £1,561 million to £502 million.

Losers from the process of council house sales are much less directly identifiable than gainers. As the council sector has been reshaped, it has provided less housing, less choice and less variety in type and quality. Those who cannot or do not want to buy wait longer for a property, especially for a house rather than a flat, or for a transfer. This can involve waiting longer in temporary housing, and being homeless longer.

Of course, it is not accurate to claim that every council dwelling sold has an immediate impact on someone else's housing opportunities. Sales of vacant council dwellings do have an immediate impact. Who

Table 2: Capital receipts. Great Britain 1979-96		
(£ million cash)	Receipts from sales	Investment (gross)
1979/80	523	4,008
80/81	736	3,980
81/82	1,454	3,912
82/83	2,050	4,827
83/84	1,576	5,368
84/85	1,343	5,079
85/86	1,260	4,568
86/87	1,471	4,669
87/88	2,011	5,206
88/89	3,149	5,634
89/90	3,276	7,428
90/91	2,005	5,743
91/92	1,419	5,944
92/93	1,163	6,579
93/94	1,335	6,478
94/95	1,268	5,896
95/96	904	5,260
Total	26,942	

Source: Wilcox (1997) Housing Finance Review

benefits from such sales depends on price and eligibility, but purchasers differ from those who would have been allocated to such dwellings had they been relet. However, the impact of sales to sitting tenants is different. Most sitting tenant purchasers would not have moved out of their homes if they had not bought – so sales do not initially reduce the number of dwellings available for letting. But when their occupiers do move, there is a change in who can take advantage of the ensuing vacancy.

At that stage, the situation is the same as for vacant dwelling sales. Especially in higher house price areas, the household which would have been allocated the property as a council tenant is unlikely to be a potential open market purchaser. For example, research has shown that around half the former council houses which are resold are purchased by existing home owners. The loss of relets is inevitably cumulative, and by 1991 it was well in excess of the level of new building in the public sector.

High sales, and limited new build, have had a noticeable effect on the public sector dwelling stock. The selective nature of sales, combined with limited new build, has led to a decline in the proportion of the stock made up of three-bedroomed houses, and a parallel increase in smaller dwellings and flats. Flats have become more numerically significant and there has been a sharp reduction in the percentage of houses. What this means is that those who remain in council housing are now more likely to be living in flats or bungalows,

RIGHT TO BUY AND STOCK TRANSFER: KEY LEGISLATION

Pre-1980
- discretionary powers to local authorities to sell council dwellings

Housing Act 1980/Tenants Rights etc Act 1980 (Scotland)
- statutory right to buy for all secure tenants (most tenants)
- statutory procedure for implementation
- discount linked to length of tenancy, 33 per cent for three years rising by one per cent per year up to maximum of 50 per cent
- right to a mortgage from the local authority

Housing and Building Control Act 1984
- tightens up original legislation on implementation of RTB
- extends scope of RTB to more tenants
- eligible to buy after two years tenancy
- minimum discount 32 per cent rising to 60 per cent

Housing Act 1985/Housing and Planning Act 1986
- increases discounts on flats, 44 per cent after two years' tenancy rising by two per cent per year to a maximum of 70 per cent
- period for discount repayment reduced from five years to three

Housing Act 1988
- further tightening of RTB legislation
- further privatisation of council estates, housing action trusts, change of landlord scheme

Leasehold Reform, Housing and Urban Development Act 1993
- rent to mortgage scheme

Housing Act 1996
- 'right to acquire' for tenants of registered social landlords

and those households on the waiting list are less likely to be offered a house. A greater contrast between home ownership and council housing has therefore emerged in terms of dwelling type.

Questions about what has been done with the proceeds of sales, and about the declining choices and opportunities of those unable to buy in the housing market, take the discussion back to council house sales as part of the general reshaping of housing policy. There was an explicit rejection of methods of planning to meet housing need and sales were encouraged alongside a planned reduction in local authority building. The aim was to create a climate in which the private sector would take the lead, and in which direct state provision would be unnecessary. However, the increasingly volatile private housing market of the 1980s and early 1990s led to reduced building when public sector building was at a new low, and when affordability and homelessness problems were most striking. Moreover, the policy took no account of the impact of increased social polarisation or of the process of residualisation of council housing.

Residualisation refers to the increasing concentration of lower-income groups, the unemployed and those dependent on welfare benefits, in particular parts of the housing market. Council house sales added to and complicated this process of residualisation, but they have not caused it. The process was well under way in the 1960s – before mass sales occurred. It is the decline in low priced privately rented housing which was the most important housing change. Lower income households who previously had been concentrated in this sector were forced to look elsewhere. Those unable to buy became increasingly concentrated in the social rented sector.

One reason why other housing privatisation initiatives did not have the impact of the right to buy is that the Conservative governments believed their own propaganda. The popularity of the right to buy was confused with the unpopularity of council housing. With the right to buy, some tenants recognised a good deal when they saw it. There was not, however, a mass desire to leave the council sector regardless of the destination – the pattern of resales after purchase confirms this. Despite widespread criticisms of aspects of council management there was little evidence that tenants believed that private landlords could do a better job. The original justification for the right to buy was the evidence that a large number of public tenants wanted to become home owners. This was a far cry from offering alternative landlords, or the restructuring of financial regimes to encourage more tenants, in a position to do so, to leave the sector.

What happens to the council sector is also intimately connected to what happens in the housing market and the economy more generally. The level of mortgage interest rates, trends in real incomes, trends in employment and the geography of economic growth and decline will all affect developments in home ownership and the housing opportunities of different groups.

In terms of the growth of home ownership and the important fiscal impact of the right to buy, there can certainly be no re-run of the 1980s. Council housing is a finite resource and a substantial proportion of the best assets have already been sold. We can expect a continuing stream of sales to sitting tenants in the 1990s, but they are unlikely to be sustained at the level achieved in the last decade.

There are relatively long time lags in housing between policy change and policy consequence. The right to buy sales of the 1980s will have important consequences whatever policies are subsequently pursued. An important dimension of these long term changes is the resale of former council dwellings. Large tracts of housing and land will become subject to market processes. In the past, the 'zones of transition' were typically areas of inner city private renting which were being transformed, by tenure transfers, into home ownership. In the next decade, such changes may be more closely associated with the inner and outer suburbs. Council housing is not a uniform product and the market will assimilate former council dwellings in different ways. Some estates are more identifiably 'council' than others. Some will have a much higher value than others. We may not see the gentrification of former council estates, but we will certainly see the occupancy of former council dwellings dictated by ability to pay, with entry costs much higher in some places than in others.

Any long-term assessment of the right to buy would have to acknowledge its significant social, political and fiscal impact. In many ways council house sales set the tone for policy changes in other spheres and the right to buy will always be seen as one of the major legacies of the Thatcher governments. Without the right to buy, a substantial number of working-class households could not have gained access to home ownership and, without council housing, there could have been no right to buy.

If the next generation is to enjoy the same opportunities of access to good housing and home ownership, substantial new investment will be required. There is certainly no evidence that the contraction of council housing has created opportunities which private sector institutions are able and willing to fill. Something more has to happen on the private side or problems of homelessness and declining standards of housing will become more widespread. The need for a renewed and continuing programme of social rented housing both to offset these problems, and to maintain the right to buy route to home-ownership, remains paramount. ■

Ray Forrest is professor of urban studies at the School for Policy Studies, University of Bristol. Alan Murie is director of the Centre for Urban and Regional Studies, University of Birmingham

chapter 19

From the poor law to the marketplace

Robin Means

The history of welfare services for elderly people offers lessons
to current debates on housing and community care provision

After the white paper *Caring for people,* and the subsequent 1990
NHS and Community Care Act, the lead role in community care
was given to social services. This did not imply that they should be
monopoly service providers, but rather that they should maximise
service delivery by the independent sector. As such, these changes are
part of the general trend in the welfare state towards what Le Grand
and Bartlett[1] call 'quasi-markets' – attempts to develop elements of
competition in such diverse areas as health care, education, social
rented housing and community care. Although implementation
progress has been slow[2] and despite the hostility of the new Labour
government to markets in health and welfare, there appears little doubt
that community care will remain based upon a mixed economy of
providers from the statutory, voluntary and private sectors.

The community care changes have had major implications for
housing policy and housing agencies. Firstly, the white paper
emphasised the need to enable all the 'community care' groups to live
in ordinary housing rather than institutions.

Secondly, it recognised the importance of high quality,
appropriate housing as an essential component of any community care
strategy, and called upon social services departments 'to work closely
with housing authorities, housing associations and other providers of

Built to Last?

Home comforts: sheltered accommodation in Chislehurst, Kent

housing of all types in developing plans for a full and flexible range of housing'. This included not just a limited amount of specialist accommodation, but *all* housing provision, including the repair and maintenance problems of elderly owner-occupiers.

Thirdly, social services departments were expected increasingly to contract out their social care activities to a variety of service providers. Housing agencies had the opportunity to become major service providers, not just of specialist housing services (sheltered accommodation, hostels and home improvement agencies) but also through expanding their role into providing domiciliary services (home care, meals on wheels), or taking over the management of residential homes.

Overall, the white paper argued that flexible care packages could allow most people to live in ordinary housing rather than institutions. It also stressed that the voluntary sector had the capacity to play a lead role in service provision. Such assumptions have always been at the centre of debates about social care and elderly people.

The origins of many social care services can be traced back to the second world war. In the first half of the war, sick and frail elderly people were often defined as a problem. If they stayed in the community, they placed pressure on women needed in the munitions factories or they 'cluttered up' public air raid shelters. If they went into hospitals or public assistance institutions (PAIs), they blocked beds which the authorities wanted to reserve for war casualties.

They tended to be a low priority for evacuation from areas threatened with bomb damage. When the evacuation division of the Ministry of Health considered removal of elderly people from London institutions, it decided 'babies and expectant mothers clearly have first claim and the infirm or aged equally clearly last claim'.[3]

Such attitudes softened as the war progressed. The Beveridge Report was concerned with developing social security arrangements *after* the war, but it was also concerned with maintaining civilian morale by offering a vision of reconstructed post-war Britain.

For example, concern about morale was a major factor in the extension of the maternity-based home help services to elderly people. Both the Ministry of Health and the Ministry of Labour expressed concern in the mid-1940s at 'the hardship which is arising owing to the lack of domestic help in private households where there is sickness or where there are aged or infirm persons and the deleterious effects which this may have on service and civilian morale'.

The extension of the home help service to influenza-hit households and those with frail or sick elderly inhabitants in December 1944 reflected the desire to avoid both the compassionate leave for service staff and the absenteeism amongst women munitions workers which had occurred the previous winter.

Mobile meals services can be traced back to 1943. Their rationale was that frail and sick elderly people found it difficult to queue for food rations. The Ministry of Health initially showed little interest in these schemes, but early 1947 saw a spate of newspaper stories about food rationing and elderly people ('How are the old folk on the rations?', *Daily Express*; 'Leeds aged on brink of starvation', *Yorkshire Evening News*). This led to a flurry of activity, with the Ministry of Health urging voluntary organisations to develop such schemes as soon as possible.

But it was in residential care that the biggest changes occurred. The remnants of the poor law and the workhouse hung over PAIs. Residents were frequently not allowed to wear their own clothes, there were restrictions on going out, and all rights to pensions had to be given up unless entry was because of illness and not frailty.

For the majority of elderly people, such institutions were held in abhorrence so that, as Titmuss put it, 'the fear of being treated as a pauper was much more real than the fear of bombs'.[4] However, disruption caused by the war was sucking elderly people who would have normally avoided such care into public assistance institutions, and they ended up in large institutions short of staff, food and other facilities as a result of the war effort.

Some elderly people made homeless by bomb damage were placed in small homeless hostels where pension rights were retained, but a clear line between war victims and ordinary PAI cases was hard to maintain.

In March 1943 a journalist from the *Manchester Guardian* visited a workhouse and spoke of 'a frail, sensitive, refined old woman' of 84 who was forced to live in the following regime:

'Down each side of the ward were ten beds, facing one another. Between each bed and its neighbour was a small locker and a straight-backed wooden, uncushioned chair. On each chair sat an old woman in workhouse dress, upright, unoccupied. No library books or wireless. Central heating, but no open fire. No easy chairs. No pictures on the walls...There were three exceptions to the upright old women. None was allowed to lie on her bed at any time throughout the day, although breakfast is at 7 am, but these three, unable to any longer to endure their physical and mental weariness, had crashed forward, face downwards, on to their immaculate bedspreads and were asleep.'

This article had the effect of speeding up pressure for change. The Ministry of Health received a growing pile of complaints from pressure groups, local authority associations and professional associations about inadequate hospital and residential provision for elderly people. Civil servants admitted the inadequacies, but claimed the war had undermined attempts at reform.

Further embarrassment was caused by the profile of PAIs painted by *Old people*,[5] the report of the 1947 Survey Committee which was chaired by BS Rowntree and funded by the Nuffield Foundation. In a 1948 circular, the Ministry of Health called for the opening of smaller homes, and for larger homes to relax rules on visiting, clothing, private lockers and clocking in and out.

The main focus of the 1948 National Assistance Act was to sort out public assistance institutions to avoid future scandals. Section 21 of the Act said that: 'It should be the duty of every local authority...to provide residential accommodation for persons who by reasons of age, infirmity or any other circumstances are in need of care and attention which is not otherwise available to them.' Such homes were expected to be smaller and more homely than PAIs, and residents would pay for their accommodation and maintenance.

The 1948 Act showed little enthusiasm for encouraging the growth of domiciliary services. Local authorities were given no general power to promote the welfare of elderly people. They were not allowed to develop their own meals on wheels service and luncheon clubs, although they could give grants to voluntary agencies. Section 28 limited the general powers of local authorities to develop services to those who were 'blind, deaf and dumb and other persons who were substantially and permanently handicapped by illness, injury or congenital deformity'. However, the 1946 National Health Service Act had given local authorities the power to develop home help services for a range of groups including 'the aged'.

The reasons for this heavy emphasis upon residential care and neglect of domiciliary services are complex. One reason was that the priority was to tackle the problems of large, outdated PAIs. However, an equally important factor was a belief that support in the home should only be offered by relatives or voluntary workers.

During the second world war, voluntary organisations, such as the British Red Cross Society, NOPWC (now Age Concern) and the Women's Royal Voluntary Service (WRVS), developed a range of services such as small residential homes, meals on wheels, day centres and visiting schemes. They were keen to develop their role further after 1948.

Such aspirations received strong back-up from senior officials at the Ministry of Health. They were pessimistic about the potential of domiciliary services to stop elderly people entering residential care. At best, they were an extra frill to be provided by voluntary organisations for the lonely and temporarily ill who lacked family support. Any attempt to challenge this view was attacked.

In 1948/49, Labour authorities like Liverpool, York and Blackburn, were pressing for permission to establish services for elderly people in their own homes, especially visiting schemes. In April 1949, Barbara Castle (MP for Blackburn) asked minister of health Aneurin Bevan if the 1948 Act could be used to legalise the establishment of such services and he agreed to look at this. But public record office files show that the civil servants were determined to undermine such aspirations.

The key assistant secretary in the Ministry of Health remained convinced 'the job is essentially one for voluntary rather than local authority effort' and a circular on the 'Welfare of old people' argued that the experienced gained since the 1948 Act: 'Has shown an urgent need for further services of the more personal kind which are not covered by existing statutory provision and which indeed are probably best provided by voluntary workers activated by a spirit of good neighbourliness.' Local old people's welfare committees were asked to co-ordinate such effort. This circular is often described as representing a liberalisation of government policy when really it was an attempt to ensure local authorities remained focused narrowly upon the provision of residential care.

The emphasis upon residential care was soon abandoned. The 1954 annual report of the Ministry of Health claimed 'the importance of enabling old people to go on living in their own homes where they most wish to be, and of delayed admission to residential care for as long as possible is now generally accepted'. A 1954 political pamphlet for the Conservative Political Centre agreed that 'we should devote all our energies to enabling old people to continue living in their own homes'.[6]

In addition, faith in residential provision by local authorities backed up by domiciliary provision, mainly provided by voluntary organisations, was soon challenged. *The last refuge*[7] by Peter Townsend was published in the early 1960s and provided a damning indictment of local authority residential care. He claimed all such homes (former PAIs, old converted houses and new purpose built homes) offered a poor quality of life because all institutions undermined independence and residents failed to make new friendships. Nearly all residents could remain in the community with proper pensions, good domiciliary services and more sheltered housing.

His most damning comments were reserved for the large former PAIs. Townsend visited 39 such institutions and found that 57 per cent of the accommodation was in rooms with at least ten beds. Many of the staff had initially been employed under the poor law system and had received no retraining. He found that a minority of them 'were unsuitable', by any standards, for the tasks they performed, men and women with authoritarian attitudes inherited from poor law days who provoked resentment and even terror among infirm people'.

At the same time, local authorities were becoming frustrated at the failure of voluntary organisations to develop coherent authority-wide services in areas such as meals on wheels, day care and visiting/counselling schemes. This created what one commentator called a 'wind of discontent in the town halls'.8 Voluntary organisations such as NOPWC and WRVS were tending to argue amongst themselves about how to co-ordinate their services. Volunteer availability was varied, with recruitment often easiest in areas with the least need. Services were not only patchy but where they existed they often ran for only a few days a week and closed during school holidays.

This situation was confirmed for meals services by a 1960 survey carried out by Amelia Harris for the National Corporation for the Care of Old People (now the Centre for Policy on Ageing). The chair of that organisation concluded that: 'the scale on which this service should be provided to meet all needs is beyond the scope of voluntary finance and their resources of manpower: and it is clear that the time had come when authorities, in spite of the ever increasing demand on them, should become responsible for this important service'.9

Despite the, apparently, almost universal enthusiasm for care at home, and despite evidence of the failure of local authority residential care and voluntary provided domiciliary services, policy and legislative changes were slow to emerge. The 1960s and early 1970s were boom years for the building of new local authority residential homes.

The full legal powers for local authorities to provide domiciliary services for elderly people (other than home care) did not occur until the early 1970s. A 1962 amendment of the 1948 National Assistance Act enabled them to provide their own meals on wheels services. The 1968 Public Health Services and Public Health Act gave them the general power to promote the welfare of elderly people, and the 1970 Chronically Sick and Disabled Persons Act placed further obligations on authorities (assessment for telephones, home adaptations). The implementation of these last acts was delayed to coincide with the creation of unified social services departments in April 1971. Previously, personal social services for children, elderly people and most of the community care groups were provided by a variety of small local authority departments.

The pace of change was slow. Much of the Ministry of Health comment about staying at home may have been mere rhetoric, hiding a continued belief that the state should concentrate upon residential care while the family and voluntary organisations should help people stay at home. Townsend has argued that the expensive provision of residential care for a minority helps to mask the lack of commitment through pensions and other services for the majority.

Certainly, through much of the 1950s and early 1960s, many believed that a major growth of state-provided domiciliary services would undermine the willingness of women to go on caring for frail and dependent parents and parents-in-law. The Association of Municipal Corporations, in their evidence to the 1954 Phillips Committee on the economic and financial problems of old age, spoke of 'the reluctance of many families to care for their aged relatives'. In 1959, the chief welfare officer of Manchester was lamenting the 'changed attitude towards aged dependants' while a colleague was warning that 'it would be an administrative nightmare if there was a decline in family responsibility'.

Such attitudes were especially strong within the health service with its concern to avoid the unnecessary blocking of beds. As a consultant physician from a Southampton geriatric unit explained in 1958: 'The feeling that the state ought to solve every inconvenient domestic situation is merely another factor in producing a snowball expansion of demands in the National Health (and Welfare) Services. Close observation on domestic strains makes one thing very clear. This is that where an old person has a family who have a sound feeling of moral responsibility, serious problems do not arise, however much difficulty may be met.'

Such views posed two questions. Did the 'family' still accept its responsibilities towards elderly parents? And did state supported domiciliary services support or undermine the 'family' in this respect?

Gradually, overwhelming evidence accumulated that wives, daughters and daughters-in-law continued to provide the majority of care for frail and dependent elderly people. An early 1960s study of 1,500 patients discharged from a geriatric unit in Edinburgh illustrated the willingness of relatives to support home care and led the researchers to conclude that 'the belief in the decline in filial care of the elderly is unfounded and an as yet unproven modern myth'.[10]

Such conclusions were supported by a series of studies involving Peter Townsend, the largest of which entailed 4,000 interviews with elderly people in three different industrialised counties and recommended that, rather than being restricted from a fear of undermining the family, domiciliary services needed to be expanded rapidly to support families and help the isolated.

Sadly, despite the legislation of the late 1960s and the creation of social services departments in April 1971, no great 'take-off' took place in the provision of flexible, home-based services for elderly people. Most resources continued to go on residential care, while senior managers and qualified social workers devoted the vast majority of their energy towards families 'at risk' especially after the death of young Maria Colwell in January 1973, which was blamed upon the failure of social workers to intervene effectively.

This brief history of the development of welfare services for elderly people since the second world war and through to April 1971 has illustrated a number of points of relevance to housing workers and housing agencies. First, the full legislative empowerment of local authorities has been quite recent and, therefore, it is perhaps not surprising how little thought was given to the housing dimension of community care until recently. But the bombing raids of the second world war provided an excellent illustration of how housing problems ensure elderly people drift into institutional care. Policymakers in that period massively overestimated civilian injuries, but failed to comprehend the likely extent of home damage, and its consequences for groups such as elderly people.

It seems we have learnt very little, since there is a continued failure to develop complementary social care and housing policies. Statements in the 1990 White Paper about the importance of good quality housing to community care strategies will mean nothing so long as mainstream housing policies ensure such housing is increasingly not available to elderly people on low incomes.[11]

Secondly, we can see how the voluntary sector has been given a pivotal role in service provision on a previous occasion, and that this was taken away because of its failure to develop sufficiently coherent patterns of service. Will the same problems occur or will social services departments learn to operate a contract economy to ensure the provision of flexible high quality services? This may be interpreted as the need to squeeze costs (the cheapest tender wins), rather than a concern to ensure that good voluntary organisations do not lose their ability to innovate and invest in organisational development.

On the other hand, large voluntary organisations which obtain monopoly service contracts in a particular area may find themselves in a position where the local authority is not able to purchase from an alternative supplier, even if their performance turns out to be unsatisfactory. It is far from clear whether consumers will gain or lose from these major changes.[12]

Finally, the history of welfare services for elderly people warns that it is always a struggle to ensure that these services gain the same level of priority as child care services. The slow implementation of the community care reforms, combined with a declining commitment from the National Health Service to provide continuing care for older people, suggests that little has changed in this respect. Indeed we seem about to enter a period of 'moral panic' about the public expenditure implications of the ageing of the 'baby boom' generation.[13]■

Notes

1. J Le Grand and W Bartlett (eds), *Quasi-markets and social policy*, Macmillan, 1993

2. J Lewis and H Glennerster, *Implementing the new community care*, Open University Press, 1996

3. Quoted in R Means and R Smith, *The development of welfare services for elderly people*, Croom Helm, 1985. All quotations in this article on past provision can be found in this book. A new edition is being prepared, to be entitled *From the poor law to community care?* and published by the Policy Press, Bristol

4. R Titmuss, *Problems of social policy*, HMSO, 1976

5. BS Rowntree, *Old people: report of a survey committee*, Arno Press, 1980

6. J Vaughan-Morgan, A Maude and K Thompson, *The care of old people*, Conservative Political Centre, 1952

7. P Townsend, *The last refuge*, Routledge, 1964

8. K Slack, *Councils, committees and concern for the old*, Codicote Press, 1960

9. Foreword to A Harris, *Meals on wheels for old people*, NCCOP, 1986

10. C Lowther and J Williamson, 'Old people and their relatives', *The Lancet*, 31 December 1966

11. R Means and R Smith, *Community care: policy and practice*, chapter 7, Macmillan, 1994

12. L Hoyes, R Lart, R Means and M Taylor, *Community care in transition*, Joseph Rowntree Foundation, 1994

13. M Evandrou (ed), *Baby boomers: ageing in the 21st century*, ACE books, 1997

Robin Means is reader in social gerontology at the School for Policy Studies at the University of Bristol

chapter 20

The new providers

Julian Blake

1988 marked a watershed for housing associations, as they moved to become the main providers of new rented housing – backed by private finance from the City

If the Labour government of 1974 gave housing associations a bigger role in British housing provision, then the changes brought in by Margaret Thatcher's Conservatives after re-election in 1987 moved them centre stage for the very first time.

The facts of the matter speak for themselves. In 1974, the year that Labour set up a new system of public grants, associations completed around 10,000 properties. By 1988, completions had increased to 13,000. By 1996, however, output had virtually trebled, to 32,500. Associations' share of the national housing stock jumped from less than one per cent to four per cent between 1974 and 1996. Council building, meanwhile, had all but dropped off the scale – with just 813 homes completed in 1996. That compares with 103,000 in 1974.

But the change was not just about numbers. In under a decade, the character of the association world changed beyond recognition. Where a voluntary movement once dominated, often helping people not catered for by mainstream family provision, a modern business sector moved into place, often providing general needs housing, and – according to critics of the new regime – forced to keep as much of an eye on interest rates in the City as on the needs of tenants.

The reasons for this transformation are rooted in politics – and are inextricably linked to the decline of local authority housing. Since being elected to power in 1979, the Thatcher government had pursued a tough anti-inflationary policy, constraining money supply and seeking out tax cuts. As a result, tight limits were imposed on local spending, in council housing as much as everywhere else.

Built to Last?

Jon Walter

City talk: housing associations have had to face up to the harsh world of private finance

There was also a determination by the Conservatives to break up what they saw as council monopolies on local housing provision. Their view was that there were too many people renting from their local authority, that home ownership and housing choice generally was being artificially restricted as a result. Council tenants had had the right to buy their homes since 1980. Yet most of the municipal authorities were still Labour-controlled: giant socialist-voting power bases that needed taming if long-term political goals were to be met.

Housing associations were to play a crucial, if unwitting, role in the break-up of council housing. Financial and legal changes introduced in the 1988 Housing Act would see councils move from being the main providers of new public housing to become 'enablers': determining local plans and strategies, but not actually building themselves. Housing associations would become the main providers of housing for rent, backed by new powers to raise private finance.

Under the finance system introduced in 1974, housing associations had received 100 per cent public funding for new developments, mostly in no-strings public grant, but also in loans from the Housing Corporation. As a result, they could charge their tenants regulated (ie low) rents. By 1987 the government, and in particular right-wing environment secretary Nicholas Ridley, was impatient for market-led solutions. That September, he published a consultation paper, *Finance for housing associations: the government's proposals.*

The plan was to replace the 100 per cent grant regime with one that mixed public and private finance. Rents on the ground were to be deregulated. Private finance, the government argued, would boost housing associations' output from a given amount of public expenditure, and deliver greater value for money all round as associations sought improved efficiency.

Some housing associations had already shown themselves capable of taking on the challenges of private finance. Most notable was North housing association (now Home), which in 1987 put together a 1,700-home development package in Newcastle, backed by £65 million in loans from the City and £12 million from the association's own reserves. This is widely regarded as the first big private finance success by a housing association.

Such schemes appeared to show the way ahead for private finance. But there was a downside: the cost of the borrowing itself and the impact that would have on tenants' rents. Tenancies on 'mixed-funded' schemes would be assured, not regulated by the rent officer. Did associations really want to embrace a system where tenants on low incomes could be sucked into benefit dependency and where the national housing benefit bill might go through the roof?

This was, in retrospect, a defining moment in the history of housing associations. As finance expert Henry Aughton asked in ROOF in March/April 1987: 'What can the coming years hold for them but a future in which they will be providing houses at rents which few if any of their tenants will be able to pay without even more massive help than at present in the form of means-tested assistance? The cost of that will virtually guarantee repeated onslaughts by the Treasury.'

Associations were torn by the proposals. On the one hand, they agreed that higher rents were a bad thing, that tenants should not be forced into benefit. Yet they realised that the proposals offered the sector expansion beyond its dreams: a chance to prove they could work at the centre of policy. Perhaps more importantly, they knew that if they did not take up the challenge, they would be passed over in favour of less experienced, perhaps less scrupulous, landlords. Better to influence the process from the inside than to complain from the outside.

Eventually, the government settled for a 75/25 split between public and private finance: a 75 per cent 'grant rate'. This was a higher than expected proportion of public money that reduced fears of the impact of private borrowing on rents. The payback, however, was the government's insistence that the state would not underwrite risk on new association developments. Grant rates would be set at the start of schemes, meaning that if they overran on cost, tenants would have to pay in higher rents. It effectively meant that associations would be treated as private sector bodies: if one went down, the government would not bail it out.

The 1988 Act itself promised greater output from the association sector. But it also required associations to end the system of fair rents for new lettings. All new tenancies would have to be assured, with rents set by the landlord not a rent officer.

Debate continued about the impact of private finance on rents and much time and effort was put into defining what constituted an 'affordable' rent. (It is a debate that has raged ever since.) At the time, the Housing Corporation said it believed that an affordable rent level was the equivalent of a third of a household's overall income. Associations and housing lobbyists insisted it was a lot lower.

For the Department of the Environment, the issue was as much about the number of new homes that could be built as it was about rents. If the new financial regime promised more homes and greater value for money, so be it – particularly, cynics argued, if the cost of rent increases would be met by another government department through housing benefit. Housing minister William Waldegrave saw no problem. Housing benefit would 'take the strain', he said. This was a short-term position the government would come to regret. As the years went on, the government-set grant rate gradually fell, forcing up the housing benefit bill for association tenants to almost uncontrollable levels.

The new financial regime was a massive change for housing associations. Another big shift – the development of 'voluntary transfer' housing associations – also came out of the same period. By mid-1997 there were more than 50 of these organisations, managing more than a quarter of a million properties. Voluntary transfer associations were all created through the sale by councils of their housing stocks, after a ballot of tenants, to associations set up specially for the purpose.

Voluntary transfers were not, however, the invention of central government, but initiated by local authorities who feared that the 1988 legislation might mean the compulsory privatisation of their stocks. Going down the 'voluntary' route meant they could retain control of the process and the new organisations. Transfers had already been made possible by the 1985 Housing Act. New provisions on tenant consultation in the 1988 Act effectively created the ballot-led process that came into place. The first authority to transfer successfully was Chiltern district council, which sold its 4,650 homes to the new Chiltern Hundreds housing association in 1988.

Councils' motives for transfer were primarily to invest in new homes and improvements in ways they couldn't without transfer – by raising private finance outside Treasury spending rules. Transferring tenants were given guarantees on future rent rises, as well as a preserved right to buy (which most other association tenants did not have). And because what was happening was a sale, the council picked up a cash sum which it could use to clear debts or invest.

At first, it looked as though existing housing associations might take on some local authority stock. But in the climate of the time many tenants were suspicious of housing associations, regarding them as no better than private landlords. Early ballots for transfer to existing associations failed. Local authority housing associations, on the other hand, were slightly more palatable to tenants.

Associations entered the 1990s, then, completely different beasts to those that started the 1980s. No more the open-toed sandals, beards and bicycle to the office. This new sector was suited and booted, with company cars and mobile phones in tow.

Of course, this is a caricature. Many associations did hold on to their voluntary roots, albeit with a struggle to cope with the harsh new commercial world. But the experience of the late 1980s and early 1990s clearly prompted a good deal of self-examination. Housing associations had taken the government's shilling, arguably at the expense of their local authority partners. They were also being encouraged to pursue government objectives like boosting low-cost home ownership. All of this made them uneasy. What exactly were housing associations for?

In November 1992, ROOF published the findings of a survey of leading housing association chief executives.[1] The survey, which took place amid rumours of a change of attitude in government towards housing associations, showed a sector ill at ease with the changes brought in by the 1988 Act and anxious about what the years ahead might bring. Over 80 per cent of those questioned, for instance, thought the Act had been good news for associations – while a similar proportion thought it had failed to meet housing need effectively. There were anxieties about whether associations were public or private sector, as well as clear differences in view between large and small associations.

The survey caused a storm, perhaps in retrospect because it was raising doubts about future directions that associations had until then kept to themselves. It was certainly not long before associations themselves were asking similar questions in public.

In 1993, leading housing association consultant David Page published a study of new housing association estates.[2] In it, he pointed to an alarming decline in association estates brought about by a new 'numbers game' forced on associations by government policy. Value for money considerations imposed by the new financial regime had effectively forced associations to compete with each other for government grant. Maximising units for the public cash available had become the order of the day. Alongside that, associations were being forced (in the absence of any local authority alternative) to house many more very poor and vulnerable tenants. Unless policies changed, housing associations would be managing the same sorts of poverty-trap ghettos that so burdened local authorities.

All of this introspection came at a tricky time for housing associations. Criticism was starting to come from some influential outside quarters too. The arguments about associations' potential for creating welfare ghettos was not lost on backbench Conservative MPs, who started becoming increasingly vocal in their criticism. Why should the government subsidise unelected organisations which housed single mothers and poor unemployed Labour voters with no right to buy?

A brief boost to associations' fortunes did come in November 1992, when chancellor Norman Lamont's so-called 'housing market package' gave them £577 million to spend on buying up 20,000 empty private sector homes in an effort to boost the housing market. But it proved to be the very last bit of positive news for housing associations before the Conservatives finally lost power in 1997.

In 1992, the critical Housing Corporation grant rate that had stood at 75 per cent since the passage of the 1988 Housing Act, was cut for the first time, to 72 per cent. Over the next five years, the rate was cut five times, until the rate for 1998/99 was set at just 54 per cent. The government claimed the process was the inevitable result of housing associations' success in raising private finance: an astonishing £11 billion since the 1988 Act.

But associations were furious. All of the warnings that had been made at the start of the new financial regime about the impact of private finance on rents and the housing benefit bill were repeated, only this time to no avail. Even the news that rents on some association schemes were so high that it would be cheaper to take out a mortgage had little effect. David Curry, housing minister between 1994 and 1997 complained that housing associations were 'crying wolf' about grant rate cuts. It was only the complaints of key private lenders about the security of their loans that finally kept the grant rate from falling faster.

It was not just the grant rate that was suffering. In 1992, the government started cutting the Corporation's capital budget: the approved development programme (ADP). It was a process that was still going on five years later. From an ADP of £2.37 billion in 1992/93, the budget fell steadily to a mere £651 million in 1997/98. The budget was falling so far and so fast that many were left wondering whether there would soon be any ADP left at all.

The process of reform of housing associations continued throughout the Conservative administration. Even in that government's dying months, changes were still being imposed. The 1996 Housing Act finally saw association tenants given the right to buy, albeit in a much more limited manner and with far less generous discounts than for council tenants. The 'right to acquire' scheme was to be restricted only to new developments. And associations, unlike councils, would be able to spend the income from home sales on providing new homes.

And the 1996 Act introduced another important change: the creation of a new official category of public landlord called the 'registered social landlord' (RSL). These could be housing associations, but could also be 'local housing companies' – new non-profit making private bodies set up by local authorities to take on council stock. Companies were conceived to overcome the unpopularity of voluntary transfers to housing associations in urban areas (because of political and tenant opposition) and to secure greater investment in urban housing through private investment. They were to retain a greater local authority influence on their boards and would as such be a more politically acceptable form of housing association. Crucially, they would be able to compete with housing associations for public funds. Quite how successful the new vehicle would be at pulling in resources for housing remained unclear.

To accommodate this change, the Corporation's 'housing association grant' was to be replaced by 'social housing grant'. At the same time, the associations' trade body, the National Federation of Housing Associations, changed its name to the National Housing Federation. It is ironic that, after all that associations had done in the previous decade, the final Conservative legacy was the removal of the term 'housing association' from official housing-speak altogether.

The election of a Labour government in May 1997 was to prove a mixed blessing for associations. Though welcomed by many others working in public housing after years of expenditure cuts and harsh legislation, associations had some reason to worry. Not least was the fact that the very reason for associations' growth after 1988 – the decline of local authority housing – now had potential for being reversed. Labour's pre-election pledge to release £5 billion in capital receipts from council house sales suggested to many that council housing was set for a comeback. Where would housing associations fit in to this new world?

One analysis was that housing associations would actually benefit from the release of capital receipts. Many local authorities would be directing their receipts through associations because of their ability to raise private finance.

But the real concern was that the Treasury would soon begin to favour council provision, because of the long-term risks of high association rents. By 1997, ministers were beginning to impose increasingly stringent rent controls (initially linked to inflation) for the first time. Not before time, many agreed.

Strategic re-thinks had become the order of the day for many associations, with some opting to concentrate on housing management rather than on provision, and others returning to their roots in providing special needs housing (often funded by health or social services agencies) or even considering a move into private rented sector management.

The 1988 Housing Act had brought housing associations into a world of private finance and ensured a business-like approach to social housing. But within ten years, the association 'movement' had effectively been pulled apart, with members expressing increasingly disparate views over their most appropriate future role. They had done their best to replace councils as new providers – but when the budgets started drying up there was no way they could meet the nation's needs. Ultimately, associations were left in a more uncertain position at the end of the 1979-97 Conservative administration than they had been in at the start. ■

Notes

1. T Dwelly, 'No Sign of Movement', ROOF, November/December 1992, pp21-25

2. D Page, *Building for communities: a study of new housing association estates*, Joseph Rowntree Foundation, 1993

Julian Blake is the editor of ROOF magazine

chapter 21

As safe as houses?

Janet Ford

Successive post-war governments have encouraged owner-occupation, but from 1979 it became an explicit policy objective

Since 1945, the level of home ownership has continued to rise. Over two thirds of households are now owner-occupiers, compared to 30 per cent after the war. To varying degrees, this trend has been both passively and actively promoted by successive post-war governments. This chapter focuses primarily on the period since 1979, when the growth of home ownership became an explicit high priority policy objective. It also asks whether this objective has been revised in response to the difficulties faced by many home buyers from the late 1980s to the present day.

Before 1979, the demand for home ownership was substantial, but often unmet. Consumers consistently expressed a preference for owning over renting. These aspirations were underpinned by rising real incomes, the growth of employment opportunities and a growth in the percentage of women in employment, which in turn increased the proportion of households with two earners. Some of the demand was also an expression of dissatisfaction with public sector housing, its increasingly poor physical characteristics and 'residualised' client group.[1]

Between 1962 and 1978, an additional 1.9 million households entered public renting, but two-thirds of them had no income from employment and the sector increasingly housed tenants who were either unemployed, elderly, lone parents or poor. One consequence was that where a choice was possible, households who had traditionally looked to the public sector for housing began to look to owner-occupation. The perception of council housing management as authoritarian and bureaucratic sometimes reinforced this.

Households often sought to buy on the open market, but council tenants were also able to consider buying their current home under a long-standing policy that allowed them to purchase at a discount as sitting tenants. Fiscal measures such as Mortgage Interest Tax Relief (MIRAS), which in the 1970s gave all borrowers tax relief on the interest on the first £25,000 of a mortgage (a much higher proportion of the average mortgage than today), also made ownership more attractive.

But demand was not always readily met. In particular, housing credit (mortgages) was limited and this shortage of funds led to mortgage 'queues' with borrowers expected to provide a substantial deposit on the property and evidence of a savings record. Lenders were frequently conservative in their judgements, operating as a financial cartel. Women were often treated unequally in mortgage applications and non-professional workers judged as having too high a risk of unemployment – despite the existence of a state safety-net for the payment of mortgage interest for those in receipt of subsistence benefits. The interplay of all these and other factors resulted in an increase of owner-occupation, but also considerable pent-up demand.

With the election of the Conservative government in 1979, wider access to owner-occupation became a key policy objective, supported both directly and indirectly by a range of initiatives. These were primarily the right to buy, restrictions on council housebuilding and the deregulation of the financial services sector. These policies were underpinned by a clear ideological stance, sometimes referred to as 'new right' policies, characterised by their emphasis on greater individual responsibility, the de-politicisation of welfare, a reduced role for the state and the primacy of the market. The importance of a commitment to expanding owner-occupation as an electoral strategy, given the level of pent-up demand, was also significant.

The 1980 Housing Act introduced the right to buy, providing a discount and the *right* to a mortgage for all those able and wishing to buy. As a result, between 1981 and 1996, approximately 1.6 million homes were added to the stock of owner-occupied properties. These sales accounted for around 30 per cent of the total growth in home ownership over the period. The pattern of sales, however, reinforced the process of residualisation in social housing that had begun prior to 1980. Sales were disproportionately to employed and middle aged tenants. This raised the proportion of younger and older, unemployed or economically inactive tenants remaining within the rented sector.[2] Larger, better maintained properties, typically houses with gardens, also took a swathe of good quality property out of the sector.

Since 1980, the stock of local authority properties has declined by about a quarter. The right to buy has clearly been significant in this respect, but so too were the restrictions precluding local authorities from building new stock with the 'capital receipts' from such sales. Whereas 65,000 new homes were completed by local authorities in 1981, in 1991 the number was just over 10,000. In the mid-1980s, there was also a switch of emphasis to the provision of social housing through housing associations. Despite some growth in this form of provision, housing associations too finally saw their real budgets and development potential limited, with the annual Housing Corporation development budget now cut to a fraction of its 1992 level.

The size of the social sector as a whole has consequently fallen and now houses no more than 22 per cent of all households. Allocation is therefore increasingly to those in housing need. This has increased the attractiveness of owner-occupation to many households as well as being the only likely source of housing for many of them, not least because the private rental sector remains limited at about ten per cent of all stock.

The building societies' oligopolistic market for mortgages was challenged in the early 1980s by deregulation which allowed banks to lend mortgages. Their intervention on this occasion was short-lived and many withdrew as they experienced the problems associated with mortgage lending revealed by the recession which developed in the early 1980s. However, the market was radically re-structured as a result of the 1985 Financial Services Act and the 1986 Building Societies Act. This legislation widened the financial resources available to the building societies, brought new players into the market, attracted previous players back and resulted in a highly competitive market.

Much of the pent-up demand could be met, and indeed was competed for, but the competitive pressures caused a relaxation of lending criteria which eased access for many new and more marginal borrowers. 'Easy entry' packages developed offering, for example, discounted mortgage rates, interest only mortgages and a series of products based on 'equity investments' that were assumed able to deliver substantial capital growth over the life of the mortgage. As demand rose, its interaction with the relatively inelastic supply of housing resulted in rising house prices.

Table 1 (right) provides a series of housing market indicators that show the pattern of change with respect to house prices, interest rates, loan to value and loan to income. These cover the period of both the 'boom' in the housing market and, as will be discussed below, the subsequent 'bust'.

The policies that aimed to expand home ownership had their counterpart in a number of long-standing, widely-held beliefs and assumptions. It was thought by many that investment in property could not falter and that home ownership gave access to wealth as well as conferring control, independence and status.[3] House price inflation was one of the measures of these 'successes'.

For much of the 1980s, house prices did rise, confirming popular assumptions by outstripping the growth in average earnings. This only served to reinforce demand, even as house price inflation stretched the budgets of new entrants. As a result of the response to both right to buy and open market sales, between 1981 and 1991 the number of owner-occupiers grew by 31 per cent, from 12.2 million households to 15.9 million. As a share of all tenures, home ownership increased from 56.6 per cent to 67.7 per cent. Two-thirds of these owners had a mortgage. Such growth was achieved by extending home ownership down the socio-economic scale. As a consequence, the proportion of all owners who were low income households grew significantly.

Home ownership as it has developed in Britain is based on the ability of households to borrow money and repay it, typically over a 25-year period. Unlike some other countries, mortgages are usually variable-rate products. The monthly cost can rise and fall as interest rates vary. Thus, the housing market and the management of the economy are closely inter-related.[4] The implication is that, if home ownership is to be sustained, it necessitates secure and stable employment on the part of home buyers. A further implication is the need to have in place a safety-net system for replacement housing costs if income ceases.

Table 1: Selected housing market indicators, 1981-1996			
Year	1980	1985	1990	1995
State of the market			
Average house prices (1990 = 100)	35	50	100	93
Mortgage interest rates as %	14.9	13.2	15.0	7.0
First-time buyers			
Average advance as % of house price	73.8	85.3	82.5	89.0
Average advance to average income	1.67	1.94	2.19	2.2
Average repayment as % of average income	19.0	20.0	28.1	18.9
Former owner-occupiers			
Average advance as % of house price	46.1	59.2	59.3	64.2
Average advance to average income	1.54	1.83	2.00	1.99
Average repayment as % of average income	17.5	19.0	24.6	16.6

Source: Wilcox, S. (1996), Housing Review 1996/7, *York: Joseph Rowntree Foundation. Own analysis*

During the late 1980s and early 1990s, each of these 'pre-requisites' or 'supports' shifted in ways that constrained and potentially undermined the policy of expanding home ownership. Rising house prices so fuelled inflation that interest rates were increased over a very short period of time (from 9 to 15 per cent between 1988 and 1991) in order to control inflation in the economy. Mortgage costs rose accordingly. The consequent slow down in the economy led to rising unemployment and the nature of the ensuing recession put many home owners at risk. These factors, in turn, contributed to a recession within the housing market as transactions slowed and house prices fell rapidly.

These developments occurred first in the south-east of the country but gradually rippled out to affect many other areas. One outcome was the development of negative equity (where the loan outstanding on the house is greater than the market value of the property). The extent of negative equity at any one time was difficult to measure and was contested, but at the height of the housing market recession it was argued that it affected in excess of a million home buyers.[5] Negative equity acted as a further constraint on the housing market, trapping some people who needed to move.[6]

In addition to the recessionary housing cycle seen in the early 1990s, more long-standing structural changes within the labour market were becoming visible.[7] Influenced by the development of a global trading market, labour market policy has increasingly emphasised the need for flexibility and there has been an associated growth in part-time working, self-employment and in temporary and contract working.[8] This typically means a reduced level of employee protection against sickness, uncertain holiday or pension provision and/or a reduction in the likelihood of continuous employment. These changes potentially increase the risk of financial insecurity for some home owners. More than 15 per cent are now self-employed, two per cent have fixed term contracts, four per cent are working only part-time.[9]

The specific conjunction of expansionary circumstances in the late 1980s followed by the recession of the early 1990s, in the context of the structural changes outlined above, resulted in a substantial challenge to the policy of sustainable, and expanding, owner-occupation. Many householders who had first borrowed heavily then faced rising mortgage costs. They often lost their income from employment, leaving them without the means to meet their mortgage payments. Unemployment amongst mortgagors grew in the early 1990s, to a peak of five per cent. While this remained below the national rate, the growth in the numbers of lower-income home owners seen in the 1980s increased the likelihood that owner-occupation as a whole would be more vulnerable to unemployment than in the past. The 1990s recession was also different from previous ones, affecting both professional and managerial workers as well as lower grade clerical and manual workers, although the latter groups still carried a higher risk. For those affected by the recession, selling their way out of the problem was often difficult because of falling prices and negative equity. As a result, mortgage arrears rose as did mortgage possessions.

Table 2: Mortgage arrears and possessions 1980-1996

Year	1980	1987	1989	1991	1993	1996
Mortgages(000s)	6,210	8,283	9,125	9,185	10,137	10,510
Repossessions	3,480	26,390	15,810	75,540	58,540	42,560
Cases in mortgage arrears						
12+ months arrears	–	14,960	13,840	91,740	151,810	67,020
6-12 months arrears	15,530	55,490	66,800	183,610	164,620	100,960
3-5 months arrears	–	121,000	122,000	305,500	242,050	152,710
2 months arrears	–	164,400	153,900	269,800	198,400	148,350

Source: Housing Finance, Council of Mortgage Lenders, Janet Ford, ROOF (figures for 2 and 3-5 months arrears)
Notes: Properties taken into possession include those voluntarily surrendered. 6-12 and 12+ months arrears are for the end of the year. 2 and 3-5 month arrears figures are for the March of the year. Changes in the mortgage rate have the effect of changing monthly repayments and hence the number of months in arrears which a given amount represents.

Over the period 1991-1994, one in five home buyers were either unable to pay their mortgage or faced real difficulties in doing so. Table 2 above provides the picture for selected years. At the height of the problem (1991), close to a million households owed the equivalent of at least two months mortgage payments.[10] Between 1990 and 1996, over 345,000 mortgagor households (containing more than a million individuals) had their homes repossessed.

The risk of arrears, however, is not evenly distributed amongst mortgage holders. Factors associated with employment status, social class position and age are the most important determinants of arrears. Marital status, household structure and region are also significant, but less so. Being a first-time buyer, or a right to buy purchaser has no impact on the odds of arrears, but the year of purchase and the loan/value ratio are significant factors.[11]

One potential counterbalance to any growing risk associated with owner-occupation is safety-net provision. Between 1948 and 1987, the State provided income support for mortgage interest (ISMI) payments to those in receipt of subsistence benefit (first supplementary benefit and then income support). Since 1987, there have been a series of restrictions imposed on this safety-net provision, the most significant of which occurred in October 1995. This was tied explicitly to a shift in policy emphasising that mortgagors should, in future, seek 'first-line' safety-net cover through the private insurance market. In turn, this market was expected to grow and develop an appropriate range of products. To date, this has not happened to any degree. Take-up of private cover for mortgage payments remains no more than 21 per cent of all mortgagors. There is also evidence that amongst those households most at risk of being unable to pay should they experience unemployment, sickness or an accident, only a quarter have such private insurance.[12] Of the 'at risk' pool, there are two and a half million households who currently lack any safety-net provision for periods of between four and nine months.

As things currently stand, the risks to mortgagors appear to be growing, while safety-net provisions cannot be said to be widely in place. This is therefore a key area for policy development in the late 1990s. Without an appropriate policy response, arrears and possessions will remain significant and the policy objectives of a large (and some writers would argue slightly larger) owner-occupied sector will be undermined.

There is a view however that, overall, these problems might be relatively marginal. Even at the height of the housing market recession, four out of five home buyers paid without difficulty. The objectives of housing policy – a large, continuing and non-problematic owner-occupier sector – have been met and are secure. It is important though to remember that the one in five home buyers who have experienced payment difficulties translates into two million households; that homelessness amongst mortgagors has been, and continues to be, a feature of our society;[13] and that those who experience arrears or lose their homes have an increased risk of both health related problems,[14] personal and relationship difficulties[15] and poverty.[16]

So the consequences of the post-1979 expansion of owner-occupation, in the context of inadequate safety-net structures, are hardly insignificant. Rather they are substantial, wide ranging and costly. A repeat of the mortgage misery of the early 1990s cannot sensibly be ruled out. ■

Notes

1. I Cole and R Furbey, 1994, *The Eclipse of Council Housing*, London: Routledge

2. R Forrest and A Murie, 1988, *Selling the welfare state – the privatisation of public housing*, Unwin

3. P Saunders, 1990, *A nation of home owners*, London: Unwin Hyman

4. D Maclennan, 1994, *A competitive UK economy – the challenges for housing policy*, York: Joseph Rowntree Foundation

5. D Dorling and J Cornford, 1995, 'Who has negative equity?', *Housing Studies*, Vol. 10, No. 2.

6. R Forrest and T Kennett, 1996, 'Coping strategies, housing careers and households with negative equity', *Journal of Social Policy*, 25, 3.

7. P Gregg and J Wadsworth, 1995, 'A short history of job tenure', *Oxford Economic Review*

8. M Beatson, 1995, 'Labour market flexibility', *Research Series No. 48*, Department of Employment

9. Hansard, *House of Commons proceedings*, 1994. 12 December 1994, Col. 443

10. J Ford, E Kempson and M Wilson, 1995, *Mortgage arrears and possessions – perspectives from borrowers, lenders and the courts*, London: HMSO

11. R Burrows, 1997, *Mortgage indebtedness – an epidemiology*, Housing Studies (forthcoming)

12. J Ford and E Kempson, 1997, *Bridging the gap: safety nets for mortgage borrowers*, York University, Centre for Housing Policy

13. Survey of English Housing, 1995/96, London: HMSO

14. S Nettleton and R Burrows, 1996, *Home is where the heart is: mortgage indebtedness, health and well being*, paper presented to British Sociological Association medical sociology conference, Edinburgh, September 1996

15. Ford, Kempson and Wilson, 1995, *op cit*

16. J Ford, 1994, *Problematic home ownership*, Loughborough University/Joseph Rowntree Foundation

Janet Ford is director of the Centre for Housing Policy at the University of York

chapter 22

The windfall wars

Mark Stephens

The mid-1990s has seen the mass conversion of mutually owned building societies into banks. Why? And will windfall fever eventually kill off the mutual altogether?

On 2 June 1997, the building societies' longstanding dominance of the mortgage market came to an end when the UK's largest mortgage lender, the Halifax Building Society, became a bank. Overnight, 20 per cent of mortgage assets shifted from the building society sector to the banking sector. The conversion of the Halifax, along with several other large societies in 1997, came after 15 years of rapid change in the financial sector.

Yet the future of the movement had looked so rosy after the war. The 1945 Labour government's initial commitment to public housing, coupled with retention of the wartime licensing scheme to control private building, at first held down building for owner-occupation. But with the return of the Conservatives under Churchill, restrictions on private building were lifted and subsidies for local authority housing for general needs again reduced over a period of time to zero.

Societies' pent-up funds and post-war growth funded the second major surge in building for owner-occupation through the 1950s and 1960s. By the 1970s, the societies had emerged as a major force in the finance market with collective assets in the same league as the banks, pension funds and insurance companies. They were, moreover, the predominant source of funding for house purchase. In the period 1973-79, the societies' market share only once fell below 70 per cent, averaged 83 per cent, and reached 96 per cent in 1977 and 1978.

Built to Last?

High street take-away: the building society sector has been savaged by plc conversions

This dominance was, however, about to be challenged. From 1980, the changes in the regulation of the financial sector which are broadly referred to as 'financial market deregulation' eventually ended the building societies' dominance. The UK government was one of the first to deregulate its financial system, with the abolition of exchange controls in 1980 being the catalyst to wider changes. The removal of balance sheet constraints on banks enabled them to compete against the building societies in the savings market. Consequently, the building societies' interest rate cartel, which had been operated to smooth the supply and to lower the cost of funds, collapsed. As interest rates rose to market levels, the use of wholesale funds to provide personal mortgage finance became viable. This placed the building societies at a competitive disadvantage, since they were allowed only limited access to non-retail sources of funds.

The net effect was that while funds became more expensive, they also became abundant. Interest rates on mortgages rose to 'market clearing' levels, which meant that artificial constraints on their availability ('mortgage rationing') were largely removed. Moreover, the size of loans in relation to the value of the property rose to 100 per cent and borrowers' income was treated more generously when deciding how much could be lent. As the economy began to recover, the end of mortgage rationing led to rapidly rising levels of mortgage debt. In turn, the debt explosion contributed to the house price boom of the late 1980s.

Building societies were initially threatened by banks and also by new centralised lenders, usually the subsidiaries of overseas banks. Centralised lenders were entirely dependent on wholesale funds, and it was the inability to access wholesale funds that undermined the building societies' competitive position. The 1986 Building Societies Act was intended to restore the societies' competitive position, while retaining their distinctive identity. Thus their access to wholesale funds was extended, initially to 20 per cent, but soon to 40 per cent. The Act also opened the door to diversification into other related activities, including estate agency, current accounts, unsecured loans, credit cards, general insurance and life assurance.

Meanwhile, the surge in house prices had unpredicted macroeconomic impacts. Not only did personal wealth rise, but individual home owners were able to turn their housing equity into cash without necessarily selling their houses. At its peak 'equity withdrawal' reached almost £20 billion in one year. Much of this found its way into consumer spending and helped to fuel the overheating of the economy. The government countered the overheating economy with a series of interest rate rises from 1988 and, in 1990, membership of the European Exchange Rate Mechanism (ERM). High interest rates effectively reversed the house price boom. Not only did real house prices fall (as they had done in the 1970s), but, for the first time in memory, nominal house prices fell, too.

Falling prices had extreme consequences for those households with high levels of borrowing relative to income levels and who were unable to pay the higher interest rates. Previously, borrowers in difficulty could sell their houses and trade down, but now borrowers experienced negative equity: the value of their houses became less than their loans. This prevented them from trading out of difficulties.

Mortgage arrears and repossessions soared in the early 1990s, provoking some limited government intervention. In December 1991, lenders agreed to limit repossessions in return for the payment of mortgage interest social security payments directly to lenders, and stamp duty was suspended on most transactions in the hope of encouraging purchases. In 1992 a housing market rescue package was launched, using housing association grant to take repossessed properties off the owner-occupied market. But it was the UK's forced exit from the ERM on Black Wednesday in September 1992 and the devaluation of sterling by lowering interest rates that took the housing market out of free fall, although a strong recovery was not apparent for another five years.

The recession had profound long-term consequences for the mortgage industry. It had devastating consequences for the centralised lenders, whose exposure to high-risk lending soon resulted in losses, often followed by their exit from the market. Building society balance sheets proved to be more robust, partly because of their underlying pool of low-risk mortgages, but also because the bulk of losses incurred on bad debts were passed on to insurance companies. Institutional failure in the building society sector was avoided. The Town & Country was the only large society to find itself in difficulty: it was forced to merge with the Woolwich by the Building Societies Commission to avoid any damaging effect on the reputation of the building society sector.

The recession heralded a new environment. Owner-occupation had reached 67 per cent and there did not appear to be room for much more growth. Mortgage interest tax relief, once the symbol of government commitment to owner-occupation, was scaled back under the Major premiership. It was reduced from the historic formula of the borrower's own marginal tax rate (25 or 40 per cent since 1988) to just 15 per cent from 1995. Further, in 1997 the new Labour government's commitment to maintaining low inflation was quickly underlined by its granting of operational independence over interest rate decisions to the Bank of England. In short, housing is not such a good investment as it was in the era of high inflation and generous tax reliefs. The mortgage industry has concluded that there will be no return to the 1980s and that it is suffering from over-capacity.

Building societies responded to this new era by adopting diversification strategies. The largest lenders established subsidiaries in an attempt to market life assurance and general insurance products to their customers, so ending their relationships with the traditional providers of these products. The Halifax (the largest mortgage lender) and Abbey National (a building society until 1989) acquired life assurance companies.

There has also been some consolidation in the mortgage

industry, with some notable mergers and takeovers. Halifax merged with the Leeds Permanent in 1995 and Abbey National acquired National & Provincial the following year. Such restructuring resulted in the closure of overlapping branches, the creation of single management structures and of common products. In each case the smaller institution was effectively subsumed by the larger. Other societies were acquired by banks wishing to strengthen their position in the mortgage market: Cheltenham & Gloucester was taken over by Lloyds Bank in 1995, with the acquisition of Bristol & West by the Bank of Ireland following in 1997.

The 1986 Building Societies Act allowed societies to surrender their mutual status and to become banks. Initially, the Abbey National was the only society to do this (in 1989). Lloyds Bank's takeover of Cheltenham & Gloucester, however, changed the whole psychology of the industry and precipitated the end of the building societies' dominance of the mortgage market.

When the Halifax announced its merger with Leeds, it also committed itself to floatation. Two of the other largest societies, Alliance & Leicester and Woolwich, also announced their intention to float, along with the somewhat smaller Northern Rock. The relative advantages of conversion are hotly contested. The converting societies might hope to benefit from a more liberal regulatory environment, although the new 1997 Building Societies Act allows still more diversification and introduces a more permissive regulatory regime, more akin to that enjoyed by banks. They might also hope to improve their access to wholesale funds, although the limit for societies has been raised to 50 per cent and retail funds still finance around three-quarters of mortgages. The most compelling reason for conversion is that it will allow the larger societies to gain access to equity finance to allow them to take over other financial institutions. In this case, conversion can be seen as part of a wider consolidation in the financial services industry, combined with the move towards generic financial institutions offering the complete range of personal finance products. The term 'financial supermarket' seems all the more appropriate, since supermarkets (such as Sainsbury) too are entering the financial services industry.

Following a spate of conversions, by the end of 1997 building societies as such will hold just one-quarter of mortgage assets, compared to two-thirds in 1995. In July 1997 mutuality received an unexpected boost when members of the Nationwide voted against rebel candidates for the board. The rebels supported demutualisation, and their success was likely to have spelled the end of mutuality not only for the Nationwide, but for other societies too.

Some large societies remain, including the Nationwide, Bradford & Bingley, Yorkshire and Britannia. These are, so far, still committed to mutuality and have adopted a strategy of 'positive mutuality' designed to demonstrate its advantages. Without shareholders to pay, these societies argue that their profits can be used to cut mortgage rates, raise interest rates, or even to give their members bonuses (akin to dividends). It remains to be seen whether this strategy will work. Conversions must be approved by members, but they have a strong incentive to agree and indeed push for conversion since they gain free shares, often worth several thousand pounds, when a society converts. The total value of these 'windfall' payouts by converting mutuals in 1997 has been estimated at £20 to £30 billion. Against these one-off gains, 'positive mutuality' may find it hard to compete. In this case, 'from self-help to money-for-nothing' might well sum up this latest chapter in the building society story. ■

Mark Stephens is a lecturer at the Centre for Housing Research and Urban Studies at the University of Glasgow

chapter 23

Hindsight

Peter Williams

What can the past teach us about how housing policy will develop over the next decade?

A second edition of *Built to Last* gives us all a further chance to reflect on how housing policy and the housing market has changed and to look forward to the prospective changes over the next five or ten years. Moreover, as all are aware, we are now writing this in the context of a new Labour government, the first for nearly two decades. Familiar names like John Gummer and David Curry have gone to be replaced by John Prescott, Hilary Armstrong and Nick Raynsford. Housing organisations, activists and analysts have had to rethink their own arguments and to capture the essence of the new administration's housing policies.

The first efforts of the new administration reveal how complex and deep-seated housing problems are and how difficult it is to solve them. Despite the bittersweet commentaries in the media, ideologically the new government does approach policy with a different set of principles from the Conservatives. However, because they face the same constraints as the last administration, their solutions are often little different. The shift from bricks and mortar subsidies to housing benefit which has taken place over the last two decades is proving to be the great stumbling block. Unravelling housing benefit is already testing the new government's capacity to maintain its principles.

History shows us that the focus and scale of subsidies has been one of the key 'drivers' in the system.[1] Since the first world war, the housing system has responded to the changing climate of housing subsidy; renting or owning; private renting or social renting; local

Built to Last?

Back to the future: Labour prime minister Tony Blair visits Southwark council's Aylesbury Estate in June 1997. Could the new government tackle the legacy of the past?

PA News

authorities or housing associations; new build or rehabilitation; acquisitions or disposals. All of these shifts, some of which are charted in the chapters of this book, have been structured and conditioned by subsidy and there is limited prospect that this will change.

It is already clear that we are not about to witness increased subsidy. The UK, like most of its European partners, is seeking to scale back subsidy as part of a general process of curbing public expenditure. In broad terms, the pattern in recent years has been one of redistribution between tenures and from bricks and mortar subsidy to personal subsidy. Taken to extremes, the possibility must now exist that we will return to a housing system where subsidy is the exception rather than the rule and where organisations and individuals are expected to make their own way.

How could this be so? Certainly, history does show us that it has always proved hard not to add to subsidies. There has always been a good case for a little (or a lot) more. This did little to bring any logic to rents charged or to challenge the performance of housing organisations, and paid only lip service to the growing poverty traps created. And while a huge asset base was created through the public funding of social renting, the enormous benefits of that achievement (which would have flowed especially when it became debt-free) have been frittered away through the *ad hoc* impacts of the right to buy.

As the contributions to this book show, another of the key drivers has been tenure. The history of British housing policy is a history of the battles between owning and renting and between public renting and private renting. The politics of tenure were intense and for years were enshrined in party politics (owners were individuals, thrifty and for the status quo; they were therefore seen as natural conservatives. Renters were collectivists and supportive of enhanced state power; their allegiance was thus to the Labour party). Now both the Labour and Conservative parties recognise the need for some balance in the system and the limits of any individual tenure. By the standards of those countries most like the UK in Europe, Britain has a large public rented sector, a large home ownership sector and a small private rented sector.

It is now argued that home ownership has reached its maximum, especially since governments have continued to reduce mortgage interest tax relief subsidy. Although home ownership does have the intrinsic advantage that the home ultimately becomes a debt-free asset, for many older people the problem then becomes the lack of cash with which to pay for repairs and improvements. With renting this is a function for which the landlord is responsible. Stripped of their ideological gloss, the merits of each tenure are now being evaluated for their objective characteristics and both individuals and the government have been taking a closer look at the strengths and weaknesses of home ownership, private renting and public renting.

Just as the politics of tenure has faded, so too has the preference for specific types of landlords, private, housing association or local authority. The focus now is on the plurality of provision and support for the landlord which can provide quality alongside cost efficiency. Housing history has been characterised by the search for the best type of landlord. Now it seems that search has been abandoned.

While the state may have resolved that all tenures and all types of landlords have their strengths and weaknesses, the position of the individual household is perhaps rather different. The struggles of households throughout history have been first and foremost about control and security rather than tenure and organisation. Households recognise the centrality of the home to their own lives and are typically pragmatic as to what they can best afford and cope with. Reduced subsidies and greater consumer awareness have the effect of enhancing market based choice. And alongside that market choice comes a more consumerist set of expectations as to what the chosen provider should do. Landlords and lenders alike are finding that there are new expectations and new demands being placed upon them.

Such competitiveness and demand side pressures are relatively new. The history of British housing has been one of supply shortages and subsidy bias. Mortgage lenders, housebuilders and landlords managed queues and rationed their outputs. The supplier was dominant, the consumer was subordinate. Perhaps for the first time in history there are now significant dwelling surpluses in specific areas. In a whole variety of ways this competitiveness will challenge the paternalism which been a long running feature of the British housing system.

The 1997 Labour government has a particular concern with tenant empowerment, the eradication of welfare dependency and the creation of choice and opportunity. While there are echoes here with the previous administration, that was most concerned with the real or apparent power local authorities had over their tenants and thus, perhaps, over local electorates. There are two aspects of the new agenda which have strong echoes in the past. The first is the question of rent control. High rents are seen as creating welfare dependency and limiting household choices. As history shows, Labour has always been a proponent of rent controls in the private sector and, although this has now been abandoned as a direct policy (but pursued through controls on housing benefit), the government now wishes to carry forward the Conservative government's belated recognition that high rents in the local authority and housing association sectors meant high housing benefit bills and high dependency.

This dependency reflects the ever more intense targeting of the social rented sector on the poorest households. The public sector used to house the skilled working class, but over the last two decades the most affluent tenants have become home owners (some via the right to buy) and poverty and social housing have become much more closely associated. This has created difficulties for tenants, communities, landlords and government. Social housing was once a part of a wider process of social mobility with households in the sector benefiting from quality housing at reasonable rents along with a wide range of community facilities. Social housing was thus associated with opportunity. Despite the best efforts of many, this is often not the case today.

Government has recognised this and is keen to see tenants not simply empowered by being able to participate in the running of their estates, but also in terms of their lives overall, gaining real opportunities for better health, education, training and, most important of all, work. Social landlords will be expected to facilitate this process, for example by building partnerships with employers. In some senses, this takes them full circle back to relationships which would have been clearly understood at the beginning of the century. Good housing was seen by employers as a way of securing a healthier and more content labour force. Work was taken for granted, good housing was not. Now adequate housing is more common, work more rare.

Peter Malpass[2] has remarked that housing associations are returning to their roots in that they are passing out of a period characterised by high dependency on government subsidy and very strong central direction, towards an era in which they will draw, like the philanthropic trusts which are part of the sector, on their own resources, private finance and their own capacities and skills. Associations will thus tailor solutions to their own areas and communities. This growing diversity will also characterise local authorities in that some will retain their role as housing providers while others will transfer that function. Universal solutions will be less common across a range of housing issues, returning us to a diversity more characteristic of the early part of the century than the period 1945 to 1990.

The UK housing system is undergoing dramatic change. The contributions in this book assess the changes which have taken place over this century, but they do not describe an end state. Housing is dynamic, reflecting the society and the political economy in which it is rooted. As that changes, so too does housing. The evidence is of a century of struggle on the part of individuals and government to find housing solutions. It is quite clear that this process continues. The new Labour government soon announced a fundamental housing review, the results of which are not known at the time of writing. While it is not likely to result in a sudden dramatic shift in terms of the distribution of households between the three main tenures, it will fundamentally impact upon costs and resources, on subsidies and risks and on role and performance. It will thus put in place processes which will work their way out over the decades to come, melding and modifying the changes which have been working their way through the system as a product of policy changes in the 1970s, 1980s and 1990s.

Hindsight tells us that we cannot predict the outcome. Individuals and organisations will exploit the opportunities afforded to them by the system in unpredictable ways. Our only hope is that the next century will see similar aggregate improvements in housing as achieved in this one and, most crucially, a narrowing of the gap between those who are very well housed and those who are poorly housed or who have no home at all. As we move close to a century of explicit and directed housing policies, is that not the least we should expect? ■

Notes

1. A Holmans, 'UK housing finance: past changes, the present predicament, and future sustainability' in P Williams, ed. *Directions in housing policy: towards sustainable housing policies for the UK*, 1997, Paul Chapman Publishing, London

2. P Malpass, 'Continuity and change in social housing organisations', paper presented to the Housing Studies Association Conference: *Housing organisations and housing services: linking theory and practice*, Cardiff, 1997

Peter Williams is deputy director general of the Council of Mortgage Lenders. He is writing in a personal capacity

Further reading

Audit Commission, *Housing the homeless: the local authority role*, HMSO, 1989

K Banting, *Poverty, politics and policy*, Macmillan, 1979

J Birch, *Votes for Homes: the ROOF guide to British housing politics*, ROOF, 1996

M Boddy, *The building societies*, Macmillan, 1980

M Boleat, *The building societies industry*, Allen and Unwin, 1986

M Brion, *Women in the housing service*, Routledge, 1995

D Clapham and J English (eds), *Public housing: current trends and future developments*, Croom Helm, 1987

H Cope, *Housing associations: policy and practice*, Macmillan, 1990

G Darley, *Octavia Hill: a life*, Constable, 1990

M Daunton (ed), *Councillors and tenants: local authority housing in English cities, 1919-1939*, Leicester University Press, 1984

Department of the Environment, *The government's review of the homelessness legislation*, DoE, 1989

J English (ed), *The future of council housing*, Croom Helm, 1982

A Evans and S Duncan, *Responding to homelessness: local authority policy and practice*, DoE, 1986

R Forrest and A Murie, *Selling the welfare state*, Routledge, 1988

J Greve, D Page and S Greve, *Homelessness in London,* Scottish Academic Press, 1971

M Harloe, *The people's home?*, Blackwell, 1995

Henderson and Karn, *Race, class and state housing*, Gower, 1987

O Hill, *Homes of the London poor*, Macmillan, 1875, reprinted by Cass, 1970

A Holmans, *Housing policy in Britain*, Croom Helm, 1987

P Kemp (ed), *The future of private renting*, University of Salford, 1988

P Kemp (ed), *The private provision of rented housing: current trends and future prospects*, Avebury, 1988

S Lowe and D Hughes (eds), *A new century of social housing*, Leicester University Press, 1991

P Malpass, *Reshaping housing policy: subsidies, rents and residualisation*, Routledge, 1990

R Means and P Malpass (eds), *Implementing housing policy*, Open University Press, 1990

S Merrett, *State housing in Britain*, Routledge and Kegan Paul, 1979

A Power, *Property before people: the management of twentieth century council housing*, Allen and Unwin, 1987

J Rex and S Tomlinson, *Colonial immigrants in a British city*, Routledge and Kegan Paul, 1979

J Richards, *The Housing (Homeless Persons) Act 1977: a study in policy making*, Working Paper no. 22, School for Advanced Urban Studies, 1981

P Sarre et al, *Ethnic minority housing: explanations and policies*, Avebury, 1989

S Smith, *The politics of race and residence*, Polity Press, 1989

M Swenarton, *Homes fit for heroes*, Heinemann, 1981

J White, *Rothschild buildings*, Routledge, 1980

P Williams (ed), *Directions in housing policy*, Paul Chapman, 1997

A Wohl, *The eternal slum*, Edward Arnold, 1977

Index

index

index